KI IN DAILY LIFE

BY KOICHI TOHEI

KI NO KENKYUKAI H.Q.

Published by KI NO KENKYUKAI H.Q., Tokyo, Japan.

Overseas Distributors : Japan Publications Trading Co., Ltd., P.O.Box 5030, Tokyo International, Tokyo, Japan

Distributors:
UNITED STATES: *Kodansha America, Inc., through Farrar, Straus & Giroux, 19 Union Square West, New York, NY 10003,* **CANADA**. *Fitzhenry & Whiteside Ltd., 91 Granton Drive, Reichmond Hill, Ontario, L4B 2N5.* **BRITISH ISLES AND EUROPE-AN CONTINENT**. *Premier Book Maketing Ltd., 1 Gower Street, London WC1E 6HA.* **AUSTRALIA AND NEW ZEALAND**: *Bookwise International, 54 Crittenden Road, Findon, South Australia 5023.* **THE FAR EAST AND JAPAN**: *Japan Publications Trading Co., Ltd., 1–2–1, Sarugaku-cho, Chiyoda-ku, Tokyo 101.*

First Printing   : April 1978
Twelfth Printing   : August 1992

ISBN 0-87040-436-9

Printed in Japan

PREFACE

With the advance of culture and civilization the structure of our world grows more diverse and complex. The lives of primitive peoples were simple, their area of communications was small, and all they really had to think about was a place to live, something to eat, something to wear, and something with which to arm themselves against powerful enemies.

Now, when man covers the face of the earth and is thinking of flying to the moon, ideas, politics, economics, and employment grow alarmingly diverse and complicated. Driven by waves of complexity, we seem to have been cast out of a quiet pond onto the swirling waves of the great sea itself. At the mercy of wind and waves, we need make only one mistake and we are cast adrift like a boat without oars facing the imminent disaster of sinking.

The universal has given us a fine boat and strong oars to navigate the violent waves, but if we lose them, we must open our eyes, recognize our own strength, look toward our goal, and, cleaving the billowing waves, gradually rebuild ourselves to the point at which we can sail the tempestuous sea.

Few people in this world know what their real strength is. Many see only the part of their power that floats like the visible segment of an iceberg and forget the vastly greater part sunk beneath the surface of the water. Perhaps such people are satisfied with themselves as they are; perhaps, on the contrary, they are pessimistic about their own inabilities.

Certainly a man who inherited a fortune from his parents, locked the money in a safe, forgot the key, and making no attempt to use his own resources, complained of no money and borrowed from other people would be a source of ridicule. Surely he should find that key and make free use of the fortune that he owns.

Because it explains the basic principles and usages of *ki*, which are utterly essential to the revealing of man's innate power, *ki* is the key to the safe. A grasp of the principles of *ki* makes it possible for you to call on the *ki* of the universal and to use the power that you have always possessed.

I have organized the Ki Society and spread Tohei style *Ki* Development and *Aikido* with Mind and Body Coordinated based on the Principles of *Ki* which I grasped through my life-long training.

Lives filled with laughing and lives filled with weeping are both possible. It is for the man himself to decide which he will choose. If you would be always healthy and always walk through life with your head held high, you must begin by studying the uses of *ki*.

I am very happy that people all over the world have read the explanations of *Ki* Principles and *Aikido* with Mind & Body Coordinated as I set them forth in my "Book of *Ki*". The present work is my attempt to fill requests I have received from other countries to explain ki more thoroughly and to offer applications of the training methods and the principles of ki to daily life. Nothing could make me happier than for this book to satisfy those requests and to serve as material for my readers' further study.

Koichi Tohei

CONTENTS

Preface

PART ONE: THE PRINCIPLES OF *KI*

PART TWO: WAY OF LIFE ACCORDING TO THE
PRINCIPLES OF *KI*

PART ONE
The Principles of *Ki*

Chapter *1* | Human Life

When we get ready to put out to sea in a boat we first check a number of things. Is there any damage to the rudder? Is the engine in good condition? Are there any leaks? Only when we are sure that all is well do we feel a sense of security and cast off for a safe voyage.

Human life is much the same. When we are born we set sail on the rough waters of the world of man. While we are children our parents or those around us care for and protect us. We live in safety relying on others, but when we reach adulthood all of the responsibility becomes our own. We become our own ship's captain and must independently sail by ourselves. Though others may give us words of helpful advice or may assist us, the responsibility of the voyage is ours, and we must know completely the ability and strength of the ship we are sailing. We must also be able to check all the parts ourselves to see if there is any trouble.

A look at the young men and women of today reveals a situation packed with troubles. What is more, these young people do not realize the situation they are in. Their brakes won't hold, they are hurling along in an impossible direction, and the engine has run wild. They themselves are either sick or spiritually on the verge of collapse. They have lost their oars, the ship is leaking, their strength is gone, and they are in grave danger of sinking in the roaring waves of the world of man.

Why do we not here and now reaffirm our own abilities and re-examine all of our parts? Let us bring forth our innate power, put ourselves in order, and make something splendid of the ship in which we must sail the seas of our lives.

Let us stop and think. What, after all, is human life and where did it come from? Most people when asked where they came from when they were born reply that they came from their parents. Those parents had parents too, and if we continue back we see that our life flows in a continuous line from the creation of man. If we ask where life came from before the creation of man we have no answer but that it came from the universal. If this is so, our own lives too proceed from the universal. If someone asks what were you before you became the adult you are now, you would usually answer, "I was a child." Before you were a child? An infant. Before that? An embryo. But suppose we were to ask what you were before you were an embryo. What would you answer?

Before you were an embryo you were the union of an ovum from your mother and a sperm cell from your father. Where did they come from? When your parents were children they were incapable of producing ova and sperm cells. They only became able to do so after they reached adulthood.

Was this ability a part of the air they breathed or the food they ate while growing up? We can only answer no. It did not come from any place, it came of nature. In other words, our life is born *through* our parents *of* the universal.

This line of thought leads us to the conclusion that not just humans, but every tree, every blade of grass, all stones, water, and air are born of the universal. Moreover, they have continued to exist since the beginning of the universal and are a part of the universal.

When a man is elated everything looks rosy, there are no doubts, life is easy. Life, however, is not all ups, there are downs too. Indeed, if there is elation, depression must follow. When these times of depression come, one feels lonely. He feels that he is cut off from the universal, isolated from society, alone and discouraged.

If we think of ourselves as single individuals, in contrast with the great universal we seem as tiny as a poppy seed. Our powerlessness and isolation are lamentable. But if we keep in our hearts the knowledge that we are one with the universal, that everything in the universe is of the one womb, what need have we to wail or be lonely? From this knowledge should come the mighty faith that we are one with the universal, that the universe will protect us, that there is no need to despond and no need to be perplexed. Though ten thousand misunderstand and slander us, if we make full use of our own strength and hold to the right belief, the universal will know. There will be nothing to fear.

A certain man made an irreparable business error, and hoping for death climbed to the top of a mountain. When he got there and looked down at the vast panorama spread before him he felt a strange emotion coursing through his body. The story goes that he came down from the mountain and through strenuous effort made a great success of his life.

Doubtless with death just ahead, the man's soul cleared. He saw the whole of the universe spread before him. His real self awakened and rediscovered itself as a part of the universal. Great strength then gushed forth from that universal.

Man today has his eyes trained only on the society of man. This is particularly true of city dwellers who almost everyday see nothing but man-made things. They have forgotten the universal world of nature. Turning one's eyes to the universal and enjoying it is not the exclusive priviledge of poets and artists. The universal will unfold itself before anyone who desires it. Those lost in the waves must turn their gaze to the universal and rediscover themselves as one with it.

Chapter *2* | The Value of Our Existence

Our lives are a part of the life of the universal. If we understand that our life came from the universal and that we have come to exist in this world we must then ask ourselves why the universal gave us life. In Japanese we use the phrase *suisei-mushi,* which means to be born drunk and to die while still dreaming, to describe the state of being born without understanding the meaning of it and to die still not understanding. To be born like a bubble and to spend our lives doing no more than repeating the process of eating, evacuating, and sleeping is indeed to lead a meaningless existence. To die still dreaming is fine, but for those who do so the time of death brings great distress.

Among today's young people some spit out remarks like, "I didn't ask to be born! My parents did it themselves; it's no responsibility of mine, but now that I am born I can do just exactly as I please!" Some young people actually follow this dictate, and their parents do not know what to say to their children in answer.

The fact is the parents do not bring about a birth just as they like. Each of us receives our life from the universal only *through* our parents. Some parents want children very badly and cannot have them, whereas others do not want them and do have them. It is not up to the parent. If it were, parents would doubtless choose to have children who would never say unfilial things or do things that are bad.

Let us borrow some knowledge from the field of medicine. In a single emission the male ejects approximately from one to three hundred million sperm cells. The number of sperm cells a male produces in a lifetime is astronomical. An individual is the result of the union of only one sperm cell with an ovum. Because one person is born from one sperm cell countless other sperm cells are sacrificed. Surely punishment should follow such waste.

We often hear the words "a chosen life" applied to people who are more talented or better looking than others or who lead a more brilliant life. In fact, we should realize that all of us, from the moment we are born, enter a chosen life. From the moment we are born of the universal we fall into a chosen life because we were not mistakenly born a pig or a dog and because from the countless sperm cells of one human male one single individual was born.

To waste this rare and precious life is a regrettable thing indeed. When we receive the priceless gift of life we also receive a commission to achieve something in this world. In other words, we must know the will of providence, we must know our own calling.

The heavens say not a word but act at all times. The heavens say not a word, but all creation is constantly growing. The universal will not teach us a single word, but acts in silence. We do not know whether the direction is good or bad. It is a fact only that the universal is moving. If with eyes set on the building of a brilliant paradise we also want to lead an equally brilliant life on earth, we must believe that the universal is moving in a good direction. If on the other hand, we chose to follow the path of evil whatever efforts we make, all is wasted. The universal is always growing and developing. We must realize that the mission entrusted to us from the universal is to apply our efforts to this development and creation. In this world are rich and poor and a great variety of kinds of work. But from the viewpoint of making efforts in the universal formation of all creation everyone is equal. There is no rich and poor, no high and low. Whatever your field of endeavor, whatever way you are headed, if you devote all your strength to that thing which is suited to you something will tell you, "This is in keeping with my real character." When you feel that you must accomplish something in a given field, you have found your calling. Apply all of your strength to that one thing, and you will sense the value of your work and the value of your own life. There is no calling when you make no effort, but the universal creative progress increases and increases as each individual carries out his own calling.

Caste aside the pessimism that holds that regardless of how much one individual may try, the great forces of the world do not change. If only one person becomes a better man, the universal is at least better by that one person. One little light can light ten thousand, which can become the power that illuminates the world. To create a better world we must start with ourselves.

Chapter *3* | Unification of Mind and Body

Once we know the substance of our lives and grasp the nature of our callings our next inevitable concern is finding a way to fulfill that calling.

We received our life from the universal in two elements, the mind and the body. We can express the relationship between these two by saying that the body moves in accordance with the dictates of the mind and that the mind expresses itself through the body. The two are inseparable. The continuation of human life is impossible with only one of the two, but when they join together we are able to manifest our highest abilities and our innate powers.

When I was in college, I heard the story of an old Zen priest who, while still young, began practicing Zen. He was a very weak man with a serious case of tuberculosis. Of course, now advanced medicines and remedies have found cures for tuberculosis, but in those days it was considered inevitably fatal. During his Zen training, the young man collapsed. The doctors pronounced him beyond help, and he, in deep distress, resigned himself to death.

He thought to himself then, "It is a great sorrow that I had to fall ill in the midst of my training, particularly since I had made up my mind to follow Zen, but if I must die, I shall do it bravely seated in the Zen position as a priest should." He got up from his sickbed, assumed the seated Zen position, entered a state of perfect spiritual concentration, and calmly sat awaiting death. But he did not die. On the following day he got up, resumed his Zen position, and waited, but again death did not come. Day in, day out, he lived seated in the position of meditation. Because he disciplined himself with death constantly before his eyes, in a twinkling his mental attitude had advanced. The priest then decided that since he had waited for death, yet death failed to come, he would cast the question of life and death from his mind and leave it up to the will of heaven. He also resolved that while he lived he would follow the disciplines of Zen to the best of his ability. As he continued his Zen studies, while he was unaware of it, his tuberculosis went away, and as a famous priest he lived a rich life of leading and teaching others until beyond the age of 70.

While resigned to his death and seated in thought he achieved a state of union between mind and body and overcame his grave illness. Those who would copy him and practice seated Zen meditation in an attempt to cure a serious illness should be aware that rather than always cure, such a procedure can be very dangerous. The likelihood is that an illness will get worse if a person approaches Zen seated meditation from the insecure attitude that, "Well, I started seated Zen because I heard that if you did it you will get well, but I wonder if that is really true."

It is essential to understand that when one unifies his mind and his body his innate life powers begin to operate and that it is the life powers that actually overcome an illness. Though we do not have time here to list the people whose stomach ulcers have disappeared, whose blood pressure has lowered, or whose hearts have grown stronger becuase they practiced in the *Ki* Society, do not jump to the conclusion that simply engaging in practice is a panacea. A desultory haphazard participation in practice is not the best way to cure a disease. You must understand that we can only overcome an illness if we learn the rules of mind and body unification and if we manifest the ultimate in our life power by practicing so that all physical motion is correctly one.

The same thing applies to ability. When we say we are good at the things we like, we mean that we are able to make progress if we like the kind of thing we are doing. Conversely, if we do not like what we are doing, we find it difficult to concentrate our mind on it. Though our body may be pointed the right way, our mind will fly off in some other direction. Progress in things we do not like is slow because we cannot achieve a state of mind and body unification. The critical thing to learn if you want to make progress in anything is to first unify your mind and your body and then give play to the highest of your own abilities.

The things that one can do when he is sincere and when his mind and body are one are astonishing. The cornered rat has been known to turn on the cat and down him. People often display powers in time of fire that they would never dream of in ordinary life. Women have been known to lift automobiles to drag injured children out from under them. In desperate situations of life or death people come up with unheard of wisdom. All of these cases involve manifestations of power made possible by the unification of mind and body.

Man receives innate powers from the universal but cannot use them because he does not know how.

Only if you learn the rules of mind and body unification, train to be able to use your innate human powers at any time, and temper yourself, can you fulfill your heaven-sent calling. How do we go about unifying our mind and body?

Before we unify our mind and body, given from the universal, it is necessary to clarify the universe itself- the *ki* principles of the universal. I first teach the *ki* principles (*SHIN-SHIN TOITSU-DO*) in the *Ki* Society and then teach Aikido with Mind & Body Coordinated as the application of them. Originally aikido means the way to harmony with *ki- ki* of the universal. However, people generally think mistakingly that aikido means the way to harmony with *ki* of others. That is why they fail to understand the essence of it and forget the principles of *ki* and the principles of mind and body coordination.

In order to avoid confusion I named it Aikido with Mind & Body Coordinated (*SHIN-SHIN-TOITSU AIKIDO*) though the meaning is repeated. Strictly speaking there is no aikido without *ki* principles.

Now what are the principles of *ki*?

Chapter *4* | **The Basic Principles of** *Ki*

Though from ancient times in the Orient, the word *ki* has been in wide use for a wide number of things from the *ki* of the universal to everyday things around us, many people who use the word do not realize to what extent everyday *ki* is connected with the *ki* of the universal, or even that the two are connected at all.

1. THE BASIC NATURE OF *KI*

As our five senses tell us, the universal in which we live at present has color and form. But what is the real nature of this universal?

Anything that has form must have a beginning. For example the sun is said to be blazing now, but there must have been a beginning to the fire. There must also have been a fire, before the fire started. If we trace the origins of all things, we reach a point at which nothing existed. On the other hand, nothing cannot give birth to something. Zen uses a term *mu* which means nothingness, but not a complete nothingness; that is, the Zen *mu* means a state in which, though nothing exists, there is still something.

Mathematically speaking, the basic entity of mathematics is the number one. The earth is one. A pebble is one. If it is reduced to half, what remains is also one. If it is reduced by half infinitely, it does not become zero. If there is one, half of it always exists. *ki* is the infinite gathering of infinitely small particles. In this way the sun, the stars, the earth, plants, animals, and human mind and body are all born of the *ki* of the universal.

From *ki*, the real substance of the universal, came movement and calm, joining and breaking apart, tensing and slackening, and many mutual actions which gave the present universal its form. *Ki* has no beginning and no end; its absolute value neither increases nor decreases. We are one with the universal, and our lives are part of the life of the universal. Since before the beginning of the universal, and even now, its absolute value exists as a solid fact within which birth and growth and death and dissolution continue to take place.

The Christian Church calls the universal essence God and its action God's Providence. In other words, God exists in this world and God's Providence is a never-ending process.

In Ki Society, we make a distinction between the *ki* we use everyday and the universal *ki*—the real essence of the universal. We call the working of the universal the rules of the universal.

Our lives were born of *ki*, to which they must someday return. Seen with the eyes of the body our lives seem to disappear at death, but from the viewpoint of the spirit, nothing disappears at all. We have existed before and will continue to exist in the hereafter. Looking at something with the eyes of the spirit means viewing it from the viewpoint of its real essence. From the viewpoint of the real essence of the universal, all of us, the whole world, all humanity, are of the same womb with all trees, all grass, everything even the clouds and the mists. Can a reason exist then for fighting or hatred? You will first be able to understand the spirit of loving and protecting all things and the injunction against fighting if you look at the question from the viewpoint of the basic essence of the universal.

Our lives are like the amount of water we might take from the great sea and hold in our hands. We call this "I." Yes, it is the same as calling the water our water because we hold it in our hands. On the other hand, from the standpoint of the water, it is a part of the great sea. Although if we open our hands the water will fall back to the sea, even as it remains in our hands it is in conflux with the outer great sea. If we refuse to let the water flow with its own, it will go stale.

Our lives are a part of the universal *ki* enclosed in the flesh of our bodies. Though we say that this is "I," viewed with the eyes of the mind, it is actually the *ki* of the universal. Even though that *ki* is encased in flesh, it is in conflux with and active as a part of the universal. When we breathe, we breathe the *ki* of the universal in with our entire body. When the conflux of our *ki* and that of the universal is unimpaired, we are in good health and are lively. When the flow is dulled we become listless, and when it stops, we die.

In the training of *ki* we always practise sending forth *ki*, because when we do so, the *ki* of the universal can enter our bodies and improve the conflux between the two. If we stop the flow of *ki*, new *ki* cannot enter, and the flow becomes poor. For this reason, practice emphasizing the sending forth of *ki* aims not only at improvement in the martial techniques, but also at facilitating the conflux of our *ki* with that of the universal. This is an extremely wholesome way to make the maximum of one's life power.

For centuries the Japanese have said that to die is as to go home, but without firm convictions it is impossible to assume this attitude. We are one with the *ki* of the universal, and to die is only to return to the *ki* of the universal. We should use all of our power while we are alive and all of our power after death. This indestructible faith is essential to success.

2   PLUS *KI* AND MINUS *KI*

For the basic essence of the universal, that is *ki*, to achieve the present state of the universal, it had to pass through a number of contradictory processes. These processes continue today and will do so long into the future. In the Orient, this dualism is called the theory of *yin* and *yang*. *Yin* indicates the shade and *yang* the sunlight. Where sunlight is present, shade, of necessity, is also; where there is life, there must be death, where high, low, and where strength, weakness. The universal is absolute in its oneness, but its manifestation is a world of dualism.

The famous inventor of electric devices, Thomas A. Edison, claimed that the universal was made of electricity and that it evolved from the contrast of plus and minus factors. Sunlight and birth are plus, and shade and destruction are minus. Pouring forth *ki* is a plus process, drawing it in is minus.

Our *ki* is a part of that of the universal, and our bodies are the vessels used to protect our *ki*. The mind is that thing, given by the universal, with which we must protect and bring up the fleshly vessel and with which we must prompt and control the exchange of our own *ki* with that of the universal. Perhaps we could make a comparison between the processes involved in the generation of electricity and those in the flow of *ki*. In the generator, the basic essence of electricity becomes electricity and flows out to activate countless types of machines. The universal is filled with *ki*, which our brains, something like electrical generators, use to give birth to mind, which in turn becomes our own *ki*, the *ki* that moves our bodies.

If one's mind is unsound, he will be unable to protect the health of his body or to exchange his own *ki* with that of the universal. The man who would polish his techniques must first polish his mind. If the beginning is unclean, so will be the ending. An improper heart leads only to total emptiness. These expressions all indicate that the *ki* of the universal is available for good or bad uses. If a plus *ki* exists, so must a minus *ki*. The individual must choose which he will use. If he would walk in the sun and lead a life of activity, he must develop plus *ki*. He must make a plus use of his mind and adopt a positive attitude. If he wants to walk in the shade and be gloomy, he must make a minus use of his mind. The attitude we will select is up to us.

Though everyone wants to lead a happy active life, the people who always use their minds negatively may as well not even hope for a plus life. A positive life depends on a positive attitude. Begin by forging plus *ki*, and you will succeed.

If it suddenly gets cold and you think to yourself, "It's easy to catch cold in this kind of weather," in a flash your *ki* becomes minus, and you will indeed catch a cold. A person who thinks, "What's a cold? They don't bother me," will get rid of a cold as quick as he catches one.

If you approach a job with the attitude that, "Well I don't think this will go too well," it will not go well. On the other hand, if you use all your strength and belief it will go well.

Many people set out with the idea of a positive approach, but a negative one comes boiling up and defeats them. In the training of *ki* we are always training ourselves to extend our *ki* to make it easier to maintain a positive attitude. If sometimes we fall into a negative state and someone tells us, "Come on, remember to extend your *ki*," we get the idea immediately and can switch over to plus *ki*.

In my home village, yearly during the first three days of the New Years, I gather Ki Society members, who are willing, together and we go to a nearby river to train. The temperature outside may be eight or nine degrees below zero centigrade, and the water flowing down from the snow covered mountains is cuttingly cold. If you put your finger into it you feel as if your flesh will freeze. When the sun begins to rise in the east, all of us strip to our bathing suits, do some light calisthenics, and follow the leader into the water to a depth about up to the hips. We form a circle around the leader and when he gives the command "down," we stoop till the water comes to our shoulders. The leader then commands, "yell!" Every one yells with all their might. After about three minutes we all rise. Sometimes we repeat this process two or three times until the leader says, "get out," and everyone goes to the shore. After this we all dry our bodies, put on our training clothes, and practice breathing methods. This is the way we begin a year's training.

Sometimes some of the members worry and ask if they will catch cold. I always reply, "If you want to catch cold, catch one. If you don't, don't." Of course if no one who went into the river caught cold, there also would be no sick people. The important thing is to maintain the one point which I explain later and extend your *ki*.

Once a man who did not practice Tohei style Ki Development asked that he be permitted to participate in this discipline. Though my custom is to refuse in cases like this, the man was so persistent that I decided to teach him how to maintain the one point in the lower abdomen and the theory of extending *ki*. So I said he might join us. While he was in the water he concentrated completely on doing as I had told him, and everything went well. When he came out of the water, however, he became overconfident and lost the one point. When this happened he began to shake like a leaf. All of the other students, standing around at complete ease without so much as goose skin, laughed at this one trembling man. I immediately made him recover the one point in the lower abdomen so that his trembling stopped. A person who constantly trains himself will not lose the one point, though he himself is not conscious of maintaining it.

This is not just an exercise in the ability to withstand cold. First, it is a test using your own body to see how powerful a state it is in when you maintain the one point in the lower abdomen and keep your *ki* extending. Secondly, it is done at the very opening of a new year so that all through that year we can be filled with *ki* and in a plus condition. In the third place, through entering the water we wash away all of the bad thoughts and experiences of the preceding year and start afresh, like a reborn baby. This entry into the river also helps develop a strong positive attitude that wards off colds throughout the year. When it gets cold, we simply think how we went into the icy river in the winter. Now, with all of our clothes on, a little cold weather should not bother us. Even if we do catch cold, this positive attitude will help us get rid of it fast.

Both a plus and a minus thinking method apply to practically everything. For instance, a person might see a few of his friends talking together. The person with a plus attitude will think nothing of it. The person with a minus attitude will immediately wonder if perhaps they are not saying something bad about him. By thinking more than is necessary about such things this negative person's attitude will become more and more negative. Some people put a bad interpretation and some a good one on the very same words. Moreover, the same words sound different to the same person depending on whether his *ki* is plus or minus when he hears them.

If your friend calls you a damn fool and you are in a plus frame of mind, you will take it in your stride because you know the man is your friend. If he calls you names when you are in a minus frame of mind you are likely to suspect unduly that his friendship is only feigned and that he really thinks you are the names he calls you. Remember, plus attracts plus and minus attracts minus. If you are in a minus frame of mind, you will think minus, do minus, and change everything around you to minus. Because minus calls minus, if one thing goes bad, everything will look bad. If you fight with your wife when you leave the house in the morning, the whole day will go wrong. Let one ill-tempered person come into a group of four or five who are happily chatting together, and everyone will go silent and gloomy because that one person's minus is powerful enough to change everything around him to minus. If one member of a potentially happy family is minus, the whole family will be too.

On the contrary, if your *ki* is plus, your thoughts, deeds, and everything around you will be plus also. Happiness comes in through a laughing gate, because plus calls plus. A person with a strongly plus nature enlivens a group of four or five people talking. Because his powerful plus is able to change his surroundings to plus. A brave general has no cowardly soldiers because his powerful plus infuses his men with courage. On the other hand, a cowardly general will infect even his brave men with the same disease. If we are interested in making the whole world and all of society brighter, not just ourselves alone, we must individually develop our own plus attributes and with them attempt to change everything around us to plus.

A salesman going out on his rounds does ill to decide beforehand that he is not going to sell anything at a certain place. He does not know whether he will sell or not, but by adopting a minus attitude that he will not , he transfers that minus to his prospective customers. He must have a sufficiently plus approach to make his buyers react positively. If even then he does not make a sale, he can content himself by just saying that he did not sell anything that time. If he renews his positive approach and goes on to his next prospect, he will get results.

A sick person is usually minus. A minus person tends to go to another minus person and says something like, "Are you also sick? I am suffering from this kind of illness. It is hard to be sick, isn't it?" In this way he becomes more minus. The more minus he is, the more plus he should seek from a strong healthy person.

Most people in a hospital are minus. Even a healthy person tends to become minus without knowing it if he stays in such a circumstance for a long time. The minus effect is even stronger for sick people. When their illness gets a little worse, they think with a minus *ki* that they might die due to this. Or if someone in the neighbouring room dies, they feel like they are also dying. Under these circumstances one must try to extend plus *ki*.

Life and death are providential. When one dies, one must die and as long as one lives, one must live. As long as one is alive, one never dies. Think only of living as long as you are alive. All you have to do is keep one point and facilitate the conflux of your *ki* with that of the universal through extending your own *ki*. Naturally the life power which is originally yours will be activated.

A visitor to a sick person who says something like, "Mr. So-and-so died of this disease, you know. You be careful," does about as much good as someone who tugs on the legs of a man hanging by the neck. The really kind thing to say when you visit a sick acquaintance is something like, "This is not enough to get you down. Cheer up."

When the man above you on the job or your teacher has to reprimand you, you take it in either a minus or a plus way. You should realize that you are being corrected because you did something wrong. If you take it with a good will and resolve not to repeat the mistake, the cause for the scolding will vanish. Later even if the teacher or the higher official scolds you, you can use your plus *ki* and take the scolding as you should. You should not be spiritually moved; there is no need to become cast down. The man who is scolding you will see how well you are taking it, and without his even knowing it his *ki* will become plus. He will lose all desire to be angry, and when he might find cause to reprimand you ten times, he will make do with only two or three.

If, on the other hand, you are hostile and resentful when someone reproves you, if you snivel and look as if you are about to burst into tears, your minus attitude will transfer to the man scolding, who will become angrier than ever and scold you more than he should or wants to.

If someone corrects you for something that you did not do, it is his mistake not yours. Do not let it upset you. You yourself will be able to understand whether the situation demands that you speak your opinion or simply listen in silence and let the thing pass. If you decide to resolve the situation by listening in silence, you will need very firm plus *ki*. Whatever you do, when you are scolded keep your own *ki* positive, and do not give in to the other man.

Because we always practice extending *ki* in the Ki Society the training hall is always filled with plus *ki*. Someone who is not well or is actually too sick to engage in practice can change his own *ki* from minus to plus by just coming to the training hall and watching and receiving part of the abundant supply of positive *ki*. Anyone who is not actually engaged in the training program and whose *ki* becomes minus finds that it is extremely difficult to change back to plus, but he can change it back if he has the help of the positive *ki* of a large number of people.

When you are finished with a day's work and are going home tired, stop by the training hall and practice for a while. Your whole body will relax, your *ki* will become plus, and you will feel good again. When you go home you will sleep soundly and awaken on the following day with a positive attitude toward your work. On the other hand, if you just go home complaining of your exhaustion, even sleep will not help you recover. You will wake up the next morning still tired.

When something unpleasant happens, instead of taking it home with us, we should stop by the training hall and change our *ki* back to plus *ki*. The home should always be a pleasant and bright place.

People who live too far from a training hall to practice there should practice maintaining the one point in the lower abdomen on their own and should make a definite effort to keep their *ki* in a plus condition.

When things are going well, anyone can easily keep himself positive, but we have to discipline ourselves to change negative to positive when conditions are adverse. Since plus calls plus, a positive disposition can lead to a plus fate.

Our *ki* is in conflux with the *ki* of the universal. If we pour forth as much *ki* as possible we can improve this interchange. We can pour forth all the *ki* we like because the supply is inexhaustible. Once we have made our *ki* positive we should not be satisfied to stop. Whether we make something brilliant or something miserable of our lives depends on whether we select the positive or the negative way.

Hand in hand, all of us together must make of this priceless gift of life, received from the universal, something brilliant. If one by one we light our individual lights we can illuminate the whole world.

Chapter 5 | The Four Basic Principles to Unify Mind and Body

1   KEEP ONE POINT
2   RELAX COMPLETELY
3   KEEP WEIGHT UNDERSIDE
4   EXTEND *KI*

Both the mind and body were born of the *ki* of the universal and were originally one. There is no dividing line between the mind and body in determining that this is the mind and that is the body. The mind is refined body, the body unrefined mind. The mind is refined and the body is coarse.

It is not really difficult to coordinate mind and body which were originally one. It seems so because people insist on thinking of the mind and the body as separate entities. Those who preach mind preach only mind, and those who preach body preach only body. Though born of the same mother, our hair and skin naturally function according to different rules. Similarly, even though the mind and the body were both born of the same *ki* of the universal, the mind naturally has the rule of mind, and the body, the rule of body. When both rules move together like the wheels of a car, for the first time we can truly coordinate mind and body in our daily life.

1. MIND MOVES BODY

We are not really conscious of using either our mind or our body, but exactly what connection exists between the two? Even if we grasp the importance of unity between mind and body, if we do not understand the relationship between them we cannot effect a unity. If when we are sitting quietly, not even thinking about our body, we manage to unify our mind, the mind and body both enter a state of unity. The reason, however, that the unity fails when we move about is that we do not understand the relationship between mind and body and are mistaken in the way we use them.

The mind is formless, colorless, and odorless, and flies from place to place at will. We may think it is here right now only to find that instantaneously it has flown a thousand miles ahead. On the contrary, the body has shape, color, and odor and its movements are restricted. Keeping these two disparate elements constantly unified is very difficult. We realize that we must make one the center of our efforts and unify it, but this leads us to the problem of which to make the center. Of course, it is impossible to separate the mind and the body, but functionally speaking we can ask ourselves is it the mind that moves the body or the body that moves the mind? Discipline methods will alter greatly depending on one's interpretation of this point.

First let us examine the view point that the body moves the mind. Can anyone bind a person to the point where the mind is immobile? Of course not. When the body is confined, the mind moves all the more. A doctor's telling a patient that he must remain absolutely still only causes the patient's mind to become all the more agitated.

As anyone who has practiced seated Zen mediation knows, when you sit quietly with a composed spirit you are at first troubled by a multitude of things that come floating into your head. In a word, we remember things as trivial as the three measures of rice we lent a neighbor three years ago. Fixing the mind in one place by confining the body is impossible.

There are probably people with the opinion that the body dominates the mind since when the body is in poor condition the spirit is gloomy and when the body is in good shape the spirit too is bright. Naturally since the mind and the body are related the body influences the mind, but this alone does not entitle us to say that the body controls the mind. People have encountered great happiness, gotten healthier, and recovered from an illness, but they have also, with a perfectly fit body encountered extreme worry and age overnight. In essence, if the body controls the mind, the mind must grow old as the body grows old, and when the body falls into bad condition, the mind must always be weak and unable to rally.

The outside world influences human beings, but the outside world is always changing and unstable. The body is influenced and controlled by the changing outside world. If the body controls the mind, far from spiritual and bodily unity, we have instability.

Frequently hypnotists tell their subjects, "You are now unable to rise from your chair," and the subject really cannot stand because the hypnotist has planted in his mind the notion that he is unable to. This is the result of the powerful application the hypnotist makes of the subject's subconscious in making him think he cannot rise. People often say that only the stupid and the mad cannot be hypnotized, because they cannot understand what the hypnotist says and do not think as he would have them think. The same is true of someone who is perverse.

Even if there is no hypnotist around, try the same thing yourself. Sit in a chair." Think to yourself, "I cannot get up from this chair," and try to stand. Probably you cannot. Try also putting your hands in your lap and saying to yourself that you cannot lift them. If you try, you will find that you really cannot lift them. Within your mind, without your being conscious of it, your mind is working to the end that you cannot lift your hands, and you cannot lift them. This is proof that the mind controls the body.

A doctor who says that the patient must lie absolutely still or the illness will get worse is only contributing to the patient's spiritual agitation. If he were to say instead that everything is all right, the patient must rest and try not to move his body he would be doing more to create an atmosphere in which the patient can recover.

Because the mind controls the body, it need not necessarily grow old as the body ages. People who, though old, are still lively and healthy are always people with a sound strong mind. If you maintain the resolute attitude that though the body is sick the mind need not be and though the body is in a bad way the mind need not be, you will always be able to overcome any illness or difficulty.

At this point, let us look at a few tests that anyone can do to explain the use of the mind in connection with the body.

EXAMPLE I
Two Fingertips Naturally Joined

Put your hands together as you see in *fig 1 a*. Leave your index fingers apart.

I.   Look intently at both fingers. If you think that they will come together, they will naturally do so (*fig 1 b*). Do not consciously think of

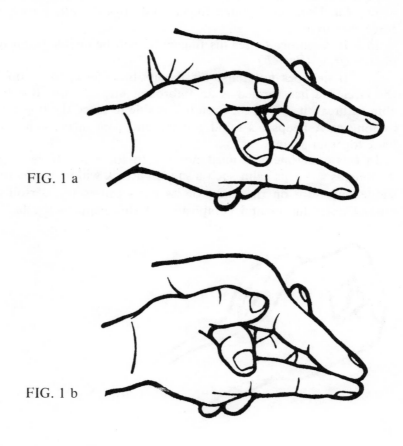

FIG. 1 a

FIG. 1 b

putting your fingers together. Leave it up to the fingers. See if only the force of your mind will bring them together.

Think of submissively concentrating your mind. Your fingers will come together in a twinkling. If you are perplexed or in doubt, repeatedly let your fingers come together, and draw them apart. Often companies have prospective employees perform this test to see if their dispositions are pleasant or sour. People who are tired from overwork or who are psychologically weak cannot make their fingers come together. This is an easy way to estimate the degree to which you can concentrate your own mind

2.   Next think hard that you absolutely cannot bring your fingers together, and no matter how long you try you cannot. If however, even a little of the attitude that your fingers went together before and will go together now remains, they will come slightly together. You must resolutely eliminate that feeling from your heart. People lacking in self confidence will, in this case also, put their fingers together and pull them apart a number of times.

EXAMPLE 2
The Unbreakable Circle

Person A first makes a circle with his thumb and index finger as you see in *fig. 2 a.* Using both index fingers and both thumbs, person B attempts to force the circle apart.

1.   If A simply tenses his fingers he will be unable to prevent B's breaking the circle ,(fig. *2 b*).

2.   If he does not tense his fingers but concentrates on the idea that the circle he has formed is an unbroken one of iron, B will not be easily able to break it, (*fig. 2 c*). Even if B is able to force the fingers slightly apart, as long as A keeps his mind orderly and concentrates, his fingers will go back together again.

In this experiment B must not try to force A's fingers apart suddenly. As long as A keeps calm such a sudden attack will be ineffectual. Generally, sudden pressure on the body or its parts causes the person to instantaneously shatter his mental composure. If this happens the test is not a valid

FIG. 2 a

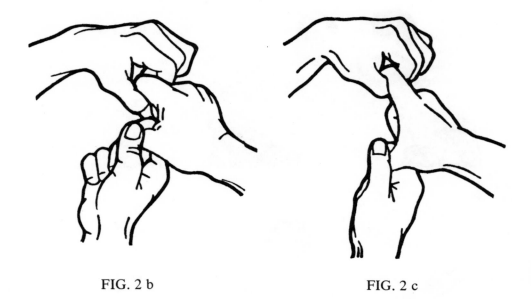

FIG. 2 b   FIG. 2 c

one of spiritual strength. In both 1 and 2, you should slowly and quietly tense your fingers and apply strength. If you do so it will be clear when you are using your mind and when you are not. If A keeps an immovable mind through several repetitions of the test, B might try using a sudden all-out application of strength, but probably he will not be able to break the circle. A needs only to think that his mind is flowing through his fingers, and it will do so.

EXAMPLE 3
The Unbendable Arm

A should take a half step forward and extend his right arm straight out. Using both arms B then attempts to bend A's arm at the elbow. B must be careful not to attempt to force A's arm in the wrong direction and cause injury.

1.   At first A clenches his right fist, tenses his arm, and thinks that B cannot bend it. If the strengths of the two men are fairly well matched, B will easily bend A's arm ,(*fig. 3 a*).

2.   Next A opens his hand out, relaxes his arm, and concentrates on the power of his mind as if it flows through his arm and leaps thousands of miles ahead (*fig. 3 b*).

As long as A keeps this idea flowing, try as he will, B will be unable to bend A's arm. If A is a beginner, B should use a slow quiet application of strength rather a rapid violent one, to see if A's mental power is active. Should B carelessly use quick rapid force, A's thought will lose continuity,

FOUR BASIC PRINCIPLES TO UNIFY MIND AND BODY 31

FIG. 3 a

FIG. 3 b

and B will be able to bend A's arm. Do not worry about this point because once you are accustomed to the experiment you will develop a mind so strong that no one can interrupt the flow of your thought. If B is much larger than A, A should be careful not to worry about it or B will be able to bend his arm.

In 2, A should leave his fingers spread apart because by clenching our fists we destroy the idea that the power of our spirit is flowing out "a thousand miles ahead" from our fingertips. Once you master the concept of power flowing outward you can clench your fist or leave your fingers limp, and B still will be unable to bend your arm. This has nothing to do with the shape of your hand. Even with your arm bent, as you see it in *fig.3 c*, if you think of mental power surging to your fingertips your arm will be unbendable.

Strength of the mind is real strength. If you believe that your mental strength is flowing out, it is though it cannot be seen with the eyes of the body. In these experiments, if your mental strength is coursing through your arm, trying to bend it will be like trying to bend a fire hose through which water is racing.

Through practice you will become stronger and better able to unify your mind. Therefore you should train yourself as well as possible. Faith is strength.

FIG. 3 c

EXAMPLE 4
The Human Bridge

A lies flat on the floor with both legs stretched straight out and both arms straight along the sides of his body (*fig. 4 a*). B supports A's head from the back of his head and C takes A's feet. The two lift A's body.

1.   If A simply lies flat or tenses his body, when B and C attempt to lift him his body will bend at the hips (*fig. 4 b*).

FIG. 4 a

FIG. 4 b

FOUR BASIC PRINCIPLES TO UNIFY MIND AND BODY 33

FIG. 4 c

FIG. 4 d

2.   If A relaxes his body and concentrates on the idea that a steel rod runs from the top of his head to the tips of his toes, or on the idea that his entire body has become one steel rod, B and C will be able to lift him as you see in *fig. 4 c*.

3.   Set two chairs at a convenient distance in accordance with A's body size. Set A's head or shoulders on one chair and his feet on the other. His body forms a human bridge between the two chairs (*fig. 4 d*).

4.   Two or three people then straddle the unsupported part of A's body and gently, so as not to disturb A's mental condition, sit on his body. All three lift their feet completely from the floor (*fig. 4 e*). As long as A thinks of his body as a steel rod he can support three or even four people. The body weights of all of the people sitting on A fall directly on his body, but he will feel no sensation of great weight. A man using his mental strength can easily support the weight of three people. This experiment helps us know to what extent the mind is manipulating the body and just how great our mental strength is. At first, let only one person sit on you, then gradually increase the number to three. If the idea of the iron rod your body has become fails in the middle of the experiment you will all fall down. Keep the

34   FOUR BASIC PRINCIPLES TO UNIFY MIND AND BODY

FIG. 4 e

idea continuous throughout the entire experiment. Since it has no ill effects on the body, anyone can try this test. Trying for yourself is a way to gain confidence in your own mental strength because no words are as good as visible proof.

Though hypnotists often use this experiment, since their subject can only perform properly while he is in an hypnotic sleep, what they do is scarcely anything to have confidence in. The important thing is to be able to do it yourself while you are awake and relying on no one else. It is something we can do while awake or even walking around.

If all you do is read this book and understand what we have been saying, the material here will not help you become stronger. Try out these tests with some of your friends to see to what extent your mind does control your body and to see how strong your mind is.

Even slight daily things that come into your head operate on your body. If you think you are bad, you are likely really to become so. If you think you have a chronic illness, that illness will probably never leave you. You must use your head and adopt a positive viewpoint.

Once you understand that mind controls the body, you must set out to learn from spiritual unification how to unify mind and body and how to make your body obey your mind.

2. KEEP ONE POINT

Once we realize that to unify mind and body we must concentrate our mind first, then we must learn where to concentrate it. It should be concentrated at the one point in the lower abdomen.

People of the Orient, from ancient times, have placed emphasis on the importance of the pit of the stomach as the birth place of true human strength. They have also, however, tended to the clearly mistaken belief that simply concentrating bodily strength in the lower stomach would produce a powerful pit of the stomach. They failed to see that by concentrating the spirit in this area one develops both a strong lower stomach and the ability to manifest great strength. If you merely tense your stomach, a chain reaction will cause you to tense your chest too, and if you continue this for a long time you will develop pains and the blood will rush to your head. We must not forget that the mind moves the body.

As the pit of the stomach involves the concept of area, it is unsuitable for concentrating the mind. For this reason I have selected one point in the lower abdomen, that one point about two inches below the navel, and have called it the *seika-no-itten*, or the one point in the lower abdomen. By concentrating our minds in that point we can develop a powerful lower abdomen. We call this process of concentration submerging *ki*, or concentrating *ki* in the one point in the lower abdomen. From the viewpoint of rules concerning the body alone, this one point is the place where the weight of the upper body should be. From the viewpoint of spiritual law, it is also the place where the mind should be concentrated. It is a joint point for both mind and body. Once you have mastered it correctly, you will for the first time be able to unify your mind and your body, and by always maintaining the one point, you will be able to move with a unified mind and body. The one point is actually the key point in mind and body unification.

From the outset, you probably have no clear consciousness of just where in the general abdomen area this one point is. Sometimes I get letters from readers who want to know whether the one point is on the inside or the outside of the skin of the abdomen or who send me sketches of the human body and ask me to make a mark in red ink where the one point should be. This kind of thinking leads nowhere. If you will repeatedly and correctly perform the few tests that I am going to explain now, you will be able to tell on your own body where your *ki* is submerged in the one point. You will clearly see that this is the one point and that this is the way it feels when *ki* is submerged there.

Though two people together perform an actual movement as they make these tests, they must not do them with the idea of being able to boast as to whether or not they moved. Always remember that the one aim of these experiments is to help master the one point. Carelessness and teasingly pointing out an opponent's negligence is no good because if your opponents is immature you will immediately upset his mental stability. When this happens he will lose his concentration on the one point and the test will become invalid. After all, we perform these tests to help us master finding the one point. If from the very beginning our minds are upset we will never succeed.

All of the tests should be performed under the same conditions so that they reveal whether the one point is being maintained or not. Sudden pressure should not be applied by the tester. Each exercise should be performed twice, the person being tested first tensing his body, and then second, concentrating *ki*

They will then realize that this is the condition to feel when one understands the one point. Gradually they will progress and should be as considerate as possible in helping each other find his own one point.

EXAMPLE 1
Pushing the Left Shoulder

A stands with his left leg one half step forward. B tenses his left arm and gradually pushes with his fingertips on A's left shoulder (*fig. 5 a*).

1.   If A tenses his shoulder or his entire body, B will easily be able to break his stance and push his upper body back. B will be able to move him even if A puts physical strength in the pit of his stomach. Using physical strength in the abdomen is a mistake.

2.   If A maintains the one point, B will be unable to move him easily.

To maintain the point, relax your whole body, and think with all your will that your weight is in that one point. Simply leave everything else just as it is. If B should suddenly apply extreme strength, A, without losing the one point, should swing his left foot one step to the rear. B's strength will then all flow away. A will not have to receive any of it (*fig. 5 b*), but B will fall forward and probably be unable to maintain his balance.

FIG. 5 a

FIG. 5 b

Many people believe that the place to concentrate the mind is a spot in the middle of the forehead. Everyone when thinking hard puts his hand on the forehead or knits his brows. That is, he tries to concentrate his mind on the middle of the forehead. All the images of Buddha have an inlay in the center of the forehead. It is considered that the *ki* of the universal enters the brain through this spot and spreads all over the body. This is done to illustrate its importance so that it is not forgotten. Most meditations preach to concentrate the mind on the forehead. I teach, however, to keep one point in the lower abdomen instead of concentrating on the forehead. I have a theory and actual proofs to support this.

EXAMPLE 2
Keeping the Spot in the Forehead and the One Point in the Lower Abdomen Aligned.

A kneels erect with his big toes crossed and rests both hands lightly on his thighs. He thinks that the spot in the center of his forehead and the one point in the lower abdomen are on one line. He can either close his eyes or open them. A will be immovable if B pushes A's shoulder.

Strictly speaking, both the spot in the forehead and the one point in the lower abdomen are important and when they are aligned mind and body are unified and immovable. However, there is another very important thing to keep in mind. When the two are aligned, the mind and the body are unified. So, if you concentrate your mind on the one point in the lower abdomen, naturally the spot in the forehead is maintained. This means the mind is also unified. This is the correct state to establish, (*fig. 6*).

FIG. 6

EXAMPLE 3
Concentrating on the One Point in the Lower Abdomen Only

A forgets the spot in the forehead and concentrates on the one point in the lower abdomen. A will be as stable as a rock, if B pushes A. A is unifying his mind and body, (*fig. 7*).

On the other hand it is impossible to keep one point in the lower abdomen by concetrating on the forehead.

EXAMPLE 4
Forgetting the One Point in the Lower Abdomen and Concentrating on the Forehead

A forgets his one point in the lower abdomen and concentrates on his forehead. B will be able to move A very easily. This means that A lost his coordination of mind and body, (*fig. 8*).

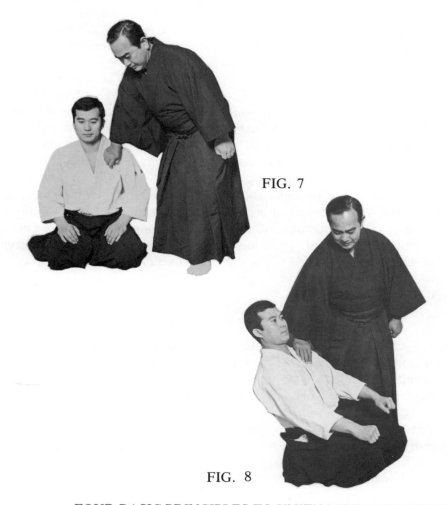

FIG. 7

FIG. 8

The above experiments show that the spot in the forehead and the one point in the lower abdomen must be aligned. If I teach both, however, people may forget the one point in the lower abdomen and only remember the forehead. I made keeping the one point the first of the Four Basic Principles to Unify Mind and Body in order to prevent this from happening. When the one point is kept, the mind is naturally unified. From ancient times people have said, "Don't think in your head. Think in the abdomen." or "A man is what his abdomen is."

Let us think more deeply on the one point.

The universe is a limitless circle or sphere with a limitless radius. Thus I can say that I am the center of the universe which is limitless in every direction. Even if I take a step to the left, one cannot say that the universe to my left side has become a step shorter. The universe is still limitless. But if I say I alone am the center of the universe, it will be a mistake. Everything is a center of the universe. A limited circle has only one center but a limitless circle has as many centers as you want. The Buddha taught this when he said, "*Tenjo tenga yuiga dokuson*," which means, "I am my own Lord throughout heaven and earth. I am no man's man, but my own." The Buddha also said, "*Banbutsu ni busho ari*," which means, "All things in the universe have potential Buddhahood." But in later ages the priests wrongly interpreted this and said, "Only Buddha is holy."

The universe condensed becomes myself. This in turn condensed becomes the one point which is the center of the universe. The one point is not really a tangible point, but the point which infinitely condensed by half never becomes zero but becomes one with the universal. When it reaches the verge of being too small to be conceived, keep holding it in your mind and leave it as it is. This movement of infinite condensing results in calmness and it is the exact meaning of the one point in the lower abdomen.

When the one point becomes too small to perceive, and you stop condensing, it becomes dead calmness instead of living calmness. Living calmness is the strongest state containing infinite movements and dead calmness has no power without movement. They look alike but fundamentally are different. You are separate from the *ki* of the universal if you are in dead calmness.

EXAMPLE 5
Sitting in Living Calmness

A sits cross-legged. The infinite universe condensed becomes A, when further condensed it becomes his one point. A condenses his one point by half infinitely and never stops. B tries to topple A over by pushing the shoulder or lifting the knee but A will be as immovable as a rock, (*fig. 9*).

EXAMPLE 6
Sitting in Dead Calmness

While condensing his one point, A thinks something like, "My one point

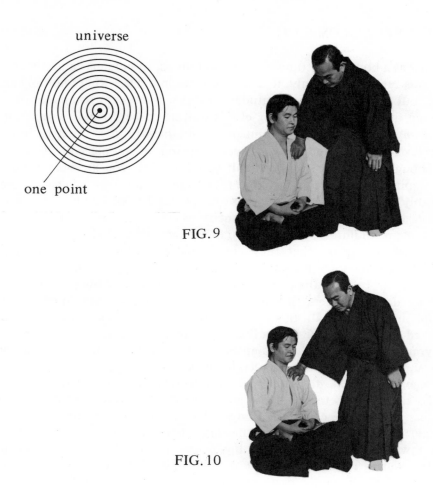

universe

one point

FIG. 9

FIG. 10

has become small enough," or "I have accomplished the unification of mind and body." Even though he doesn't and shouldn't move any part of his body, B will be able to detect that A has stopped condensing his one point. The eyelashes or cheeks will begin to move a little or a dark shadow will be cast across his face. Each person has his own way of expressing this but it is always discernible. At that instant B will be able to push A over by the shoulder,(*fig. 10*).

In conclusion the one point in the lower abdomen is not a tangible point but a point infinitely condensed. The one point in the lower abdomen is important but don't stop your mind there. While condensing to infinite smallness, if it becomes too small to perceive, just leave it as it is. *Ki* is the infinite gathering of infinitely small particles. When the mind is refined to this degree, for the first time one can become one with the universal.

Once you understand that you have the center of the universe in your abdomen, try to begin every action from this point and absorb everything and every influence into this point. Then you will be able to keep coordination of mind and body in your daily life.

FOUR BASIC PRINCIPLES TO UNIFY MIND AND BODY 41

3.   RELAX COMPLETELY

Just as a bow kept strung loses its usefulness, so humans cannot stand continuous tension. Certainly, it is easy to relax in a place where nothing annoys you, but in the bustling vicissitudes of this world where you have not finished one thing before something else is waiting to be done, it is impossible to be always in a relaxing environment. Consequently, it is essential to be able to relax both mind and body, as needs demand, in any place at all.

Though, of course, it is difficult to relax when you are busy, some people's spirits are in such a rush that they cannot relax even when they are in a suitably relaxing atmosphere. These people tend to be highly nervous and to tire easily. In the face of some momentous event they are likely to tense and tighten up. Children before an entrance exam often find themselves unable to answer questions that they could answer under normal circumstance. Athletes before some big game sometimes tighten up and do poorly. All of this happens because the people involved do not know how to relax.

Why do people feel that it is impossible to relax when something big is happening? First of all, this notion arises from the illusion that when one is relaxed he is weak. The fact is that if you relax properly you are very strong, as you will see from the examples we shall mention later. We relax at important, trying times because relaxing makes us strong.

Secondly people do not know how to relax and feel that they cannot.

To relax means to be at ease and leave things in their natural condition. We can relax if we can make things settle down in their proper places. The proper place for the weight of the upper body to settle is the one point in the lower abdomen. First find the place, the one point where the upper body's weight must settle. Settle it there, and relax the upper body, and the weight of all the other parts of the body will settle down at their proper places for a state of over-all relaxation. If a man does not know the house to which he must return, even if you tell him to go home, he can't. If you do not know the place in which to settle your strength, even if we tell you to relax, you can't.

When you are trying to relax, and you don't know where to settle your strength, your strength remains in some part of your body. If you try to relax the shoulders, the belly is tense. If you try to relax your belly, your head becomes tense. In this way some part of your body is always tense and you cannot relax completely.

There is an old story about a magic pot. One merchant came to sell an old pot. People complained because the pot was very expensive. The merchant said, "No, it is not expensive at all. It is a magic pot." "What kind of magic can it play?" "Put anything you like in the pot." They threw whatever they had around into the pot and it all vanished. It was truly a magic pot.

Such pots must be very useful. We all have such a magic pot in the one point in the lower abdomen. This is an infinitely small point which can engulf everything. For example, even if someone spreads false rumors about you, you need not lose your temper. By throwing your anger away into your one point, you need not do something heatedly that you would later regret. Nor need you repress it, which only means the anger will come out later. If you absorb your anger and the irritations and disappointments of everyday life in your one point you can truly throw them away and be rid of such cumbersome emotional baggage. If you live this way even though lightning strikes beside you, you will not be shaken up by the sound and the flash of light. They will be instantly absorbed into the one point and be extinguished.

As one tries to improve his one point in daily life, one should be able to maintain a perpetually relaxed state of mind and body. He will develop a mind which is immovable even though the world around collapses, and a mind which is as vast as the ocean which can engulf everything and remain unpolluted.

EXAMPLE 1.
Both Hands Pulled Down

A stands and B and C hold A's hands with both hands and try to pull him down. If A puts strength in his arms, he will be pulled down, (*fig. 11 a*).

Next A relaxes his arms completely thinking of absorbing their power into the magic pot into his one point in the lower abdomen. B and C will not be able to pull A down however hard they try. A can even stand up and lower his hip with B and C hanging on the arms, (*fig. 11 b*).

Even if you actually receive power from B and C, all you have to do is to absorb it into your one point. By absorbing all disturbing and irksome things in this world into the one point, you can overcome all difficulties in this life.

FIG. 11a   FIG. 11b

EXAMPLE 2.
Relaxation with and without One Point

A stands. B tries to push A's hand toward his shoulder with both hands. If A keeps one point and relaxes, B will not be able to budge him even a little. This is the true state of relaxation and is the strongest state, (*fig. 12 a*). Next A relaxes thinking of the top of his head or concentrating on the forehead. B will be able to push A's hand upward easily and A will lose his balance. This is the false state of relaxation, the weakest state, (*fig. 12 b*).

People in the world usually believe that relaxation means loss of power. That is why they cannot relax in an emergency. They tense their body. You will realize the importance of relaxation in an emergency for the first time when you realize that relaxation is the strongest state. From ancient times all the great men never got upset in an emergency and were always relaxed because they knew the true relaxation. We, too, can achieve it if we want.

Recent medical reports say that 80% of modern disease are due to nervous problems. Stresses, irritations, anger, and depression make the fine veins contract and disturb the manifestation of the life power causing various diseases. One should lead a happy healthy life by keeping the one point, relaxing completely, activating the highest life power, and thereby keeping away all diseases. To relax completely is the second of the Four Basic Principles to Unify Mind and Body.

FIG. 12a

FIG. 12b

4. KEEP WEIGHT UNDERSIDE

The weight of every object naturally settles at its lowest point. Since the body of a man is also an object, if he relaxes completely, the weight of every part should naturally be settled at the lowest point. Living calmness is a state where the weight of an object naturally settles underside. So, if a man relaxes completely he can always remain calm. This is the third of the Four Basic Principles. If we keep one point, we can relax. If we relax, the weight of every part of our body is at the lowest point. The first, second and the third of the Four Basic Principles are inseparable.

EXAMPLE 1
The Heavy Arm

A thrusts his right arm straight out in front of him, and using only one hand, B attempts to push A's forearm upward.

1.   If A relaxes his arm and thinks of the lower edge of it (heavy line in *fig. 13 a*), B will not be able to push it up easily.

2.   If A thinks of the upper edge of his arm, (heavy line in *fig. 13 b*), B will be able to easily push A's arm upward.

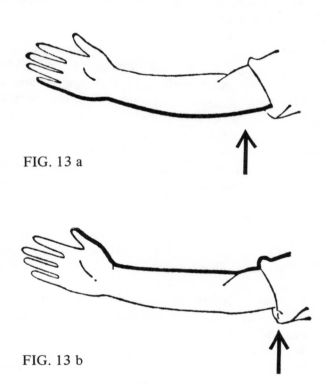

FIG. 13 a

FIG. 13 b

By simply changing the location in which we concentrate our mind we can make our arm light or heavy. The same is true of the body as a whole. If we concentrate on our heads, our entire body becomes easy to lift. If we concentrate on the lower parts of our body it becomes heavy and difficult to lift.

When I was in Hawaii, I was asked to explain and give a demonstration of aikido with mind and body coordinated for a convention of doctors from all over the world. When I was finished, a number of doctors gathered around me and said, "You are said to be able to change your pulse by using your will power, but the automatic nerves control the pulse. You should not be able to willfully change it at all. Won't you let us measure your pulse action?" Some of the doctors took out their watches and actually took my pulse count. In the first minute it was 91, the second time they took it is was 70, and the third it was 81. The doctors agreed that it certainly did change and asked me how I did it.

Actually it is no great problem. Anyone when angry or surprised has a faster pulse rate. Likewise, anyone when calm, as we are when we first wake up in the morning, has a slow pulse rate. When we want to speed up our pulse rate all we do is concentrate deeply on being angry, and it will increase. On the other hand, if we concentrate on being in the state we are in when we first awaken, our pulse rate will slow down. When I explained this to the doctors, they all immediately tried it, but none of them was able to change his pulse.

One then asked, "I'm calm now. How am I supposed to convince myself that I am angry?" I replied, "Practice *Ki* and reach the stage where you can use your own mind freely." They all laughed and agreed. The difficult thing is not changing your pulse rate but freely changing your own mind. It is easier to speed up your pulse rate than to slow it down when it is fast, but slowing it down is what you should aim for because if you can do that you will be able to laugh off any scare or shock.

If you concentrate with all your might on raising your blood to your head, your pulse rate will speed up. If you relax and think hard about your blood flowing downward, your pulse rate will slow down. It depends on how you hold your mind.

EXAMPLE 2
The Unraisable Face

A kneels properly, and B takes A's chin in his hand and attempts to raise A's head, (*fig. 14*). Were the weight in the lower part of A's chin, B could not easily lift it.

Were B to attempt to raise A's hands from his knees he could not. If he were to attempt to lift A's knees he could not do it easily because the weight of A's knees is in their lowest areas. If your mind is calm, your body will naturally be in this condition. You must learn that a natural position is not only the most correct, but also the strongest. If, though you seem calm,

FIG. 14

your head, your hands, and your knees can be raised, you only look calm but are not really.

EXAMPLE 3
The Weight in the Lowest Part of the Arm

A takes a half step forward with his right foot and extends his right arm in front of him. Though B tries to force A's arm down, A will not let him.

1.   It is impossible for B to strike A's arm down though A's arm tensed because the weight in B's arm is set in the arm's upper side, (*fig. 15 a*).

FIG. 15a

FIG. 15b.

FOUR BASIC PRINCIPLES TO UNIFY MIND AND BODY   47

2.   B can strike A's arm down if he completely relaxes his own, and concentrates on his arm's weight being in the lowest part of the arm. When he does this, the weight of the arm will charge the entire arm, which will naturally descend easily bringing A's arm down too (*fig. 15 b*), regardless of how much strength A puts into his arm or how much he attempts to resist. The important thing is that B must keep the weight of his arm in that arm's lowest part.

In aikido with mind and body coordinated, even in merely striking down one arm, it should be done naturally with the weight underside. This is part of the attitude that each raising of the hand and extending of the foot should be done naturally and according to the rules of the universal. For this reason everything that we do in aikido, though it seems very comfortable and easy to the observer, actually has terrific power.

If you relax keeping the weight of your body at its lowest part, naturally your mind calms down. The brain is always working while you are alive, you cannot eliminate the waves of the mind. It is impossible not to think anything. The waves of the brain, however, can be calmed down by half infinitely. When the waves are calmed down infinitely toward zero, it is called concentration. "Think nothing" means concentration or calmness. It is a state of mind like a clear water surface which reflects, clearly and without error, everything and every phenomenon of the world. In this complicated modern age, it must be valuable to learn how to acquire calmness of the mind which can distinguish right from wrong clearly.

5.   EXTEND KI

"Extend Ki" is the fourth of the Four Basic Principles to Unify Mind and Body. Our lives are a part of the *ki* of the universal. Just like the amount of sea water held in our hands, we surround a part of the *ki* of the universal with our body and say, "This is I." When the *ki* in our body interchanges with the *ki* of the universal, we are alive. When we extend *ki*, a new supply of *ki* flows into our body and the interchange is improved. It is our natural state that *ki* is extending as long as we are alive. If we keep one point, relax, or keep weight underside, they are all the same state in which *ki* is extending.

Do experiments with the "unbendable arm." The Four Basic Principles cannot be separated. If one of them is satisfied, all the other three are naturally maintained. If one of them is lost, the other three are also lost. The first and fourth principles are principles of the mind and the second and the third, principles of the body. When the principles of both go together like wheels of a car, for the first time one can maintain the state of mind and body coordination in his daily life.

Chapter 6 | Coordination of Mind and Body in Daily Life

It is rather easy to unify mind and body when one does not move his body. The difficulty is coordination of mind and body while moving. If you train yourself in the mountains for ten or twenty years and achieve coordination of mind and body, if it is disturbed when you come down to the city, it is of no use. We all have to work in order to live. We should train ourselves so that whatever movements we make, we can still keep coordination of mind and body. The mind has its own principles and the body, likewise Tohei style *Ki* exercises exist in order to examine closely all the movements according to the Four Basic Principles to Unify Mind and Body and to train the mind and the body so that every action is naturally according to the laws of the universal. There are several examples.

EXAMPLE 1
The Unbendable Arm

We explained the unbendable arm before, but this time A, without concentrating on his mental strength's flowing a thousand miles into space, merely thrusts his right hand out. If A maintains the one point in the lower abdomen, B, try as he may, will be unable to bend A's arm. In other words, if you maintain the one point, even if you do not think that your mental strength is flooding forth, *ki* will be flowing out from your entire body. If your opponent can bend your arm your *ki* has stopped flowing and you are not maintaining the one point.
In daily life, we can't always be thinking about power flowing forth a thousand miles ahead from our hands or from our feet. Moreover, it is unnecessary to constantly have this on our minds, because if we maintain the one point we are always in a condition in which *ki* is flowing out from our whole body. If our *ki* is not flowing out from our body, no matter how much we try, we will be unable to maintain the one point. Though the words may be different, extending *ki* and maintaining the one point are an indivisible unit.

I only teach one point, which is always the same one point. However busy you are, you can do it in your daily life if you have a will. The busier one is, the more one should practice it.

EXAMPLE 2
The Opponent Pushes You Back by the Wrist

A stands in the same position, with his left hand out and his left wrist well bent. B, using one hand, attempts to push the back of A's hand in the direction of A's shoulder,(*fig. 16*).

If A puts up a great resistance, B will either push him backwards or bend his arm at the elbow. If A tenses his arm, B will find it all the easier to push him back. Because you are standing so that though your opponent pushes your shoulder he cannot break your posture, if you have your left arm in the outthrust unbendable arm position you should be so stable that your opponent cannot move you. However, when you begin to raise your left arm the idea of "raising" comes into your mind, and the weight of your arm shifts upward. Without knowing it, you tense your arm, and you lose concentration on the one point. Moreover, when you bend your arm, you draw in *ki*. Aikido with mind and body coordinated techniques frquently demands that we keep *ki* flowing forth and bend our wrists. The shoulder has joints; movement in the arm should have no effect on the one point. If you maintain the one point and raise your arm naturally, the man's weight should stay in the lower section, and *ki* should be constantly outflowing. If when you bend your wrist you do not draw *ki* in but thrust the back of your hand out so that *ki* is still flowing outward, the opponent will not be able to move you.

FIG. 16   FIG. 17

EXAMPLE 3
Standing on One Leg.

A stands in the position in *fig 16* with his left arm outstreched and with his left thigh raised up high (*fig. 17*).

B attempts to push A's left hand in the direction of A's shoulder. A person who puts up a great resistance will stagger backwards; some people stagger and fall back just from raising their thighs, even if no one pushes them.

If you are conscious of raising your thigh, your one point will rise, your arm becomes tense, and you will lose your balance. Let the muscles in the base of your thigh do the lifting. The action of raising should have nothing to do with the one point. If you maintain the one point, relax your arm completely, and raise your thigh, your opponent will not be able to move you. If you are alone, if you do as we just said, you will be able to stand on one leg without trembling.

EXAMPLE 4
Standing With Both Hands Raised

A stands with both legs one half step apart and with both hands raised. B presses quietly on the center part of A's chest,(*fig. 18*).

FIG. 18

Once again, A is likely to stagger backwards. If, as he raises his hands, his one point also rises, he will fall back.

If someone with a knife or a pistol attempts to hold you up you can rapidly dodge out of the line of fire and take away your assailant's weapon if when you raise your hands you maintain the one point and assume a stable posture from which you can freely move your hips. The danger lies, of course, in allowing the one point to rise so that you cannot freely manipulate your hips. In aikido with mind and body coordinated, the use of the hips is extremely important, but to use them freely and powerfully you must maintain the one point. Whether you raise or lower your arms or swing them, the one point must remain stable and unmoved.

In all of these experiments, if you are not properly prepared, though you have a firm grip on the one point, if you move your hands and feet just a little, you may lose the one point. It is the same as being on a mountaintop where your mind and body are unified and then losing that unification as you descend the mountain and enter your own village. The reason behind this is a lack of knowledge of the proper way to maintain the one point. If you practice doing so carefully, you will be able to remain in a state of mind and body unification whatever you are doing.

EXAMPLE 5
Stooping

Up to this point we have had A standing up straight and maintaining the one point, but human beings must also be able to stoop over or bend backwards without losing the one point.

A stoops over as if he were tying his shoe. B attempts to push A's hips forward,(*fig. 19*).

1. If A tenses his shoulders and forgets about the one point, B will be able to push him over forward.

2. If, on the other hand, A bends over and maintains the one point without tensing his shoulders, if B pushes him slightly, he will remain unmoved, and if B gives him a hard push, he will be able to stand and walk away without falling over.

FIG. 19

EXAMPLE 6
Bending Backward

A stands with his left foot one step forward and leans backward with the upper part of his body. B pushes on A's left shoulder and attempts to push him down,*(fig. 20)*.

1. If A tenses the area around the shoulders, B can easily push him down.

2. B will not be able to push A down easily, however, if A relaxes his shoulders and maintains the one point.

In both examples 5 and 6, whether bending forward or backward as long as A maintains the one point, *ki* courses through his body and gives it the strength and resiliency of young bamboo. But if A tenses his shoulders, he loses the one point and his strength and resilient power disert him and leave him like broken bamboo.

FIG. 20

EXAMPLE 7
A Leaning on B

B bends over half way at the waist. A puts both arms on B's back and leans on him,*(fig. 21a)*. If sufficient of A's weight falls on B's back, B will fall flat to the floor. Should A also fall over forward, it would be proof that he had lost the one point. Had he not lost it, even though he applied his weight to B's back and even though his arms were lowered, his body's weight would have been in the one point and he would not have had to stagger,*(fig. 21 b)* .

If someone who is leaning on a wall falls should the wall happen to crumble, or similarly if someone leaning on a bridge railing should plunge into the river if the railing gives way, it would be because they were not maintaining the one point. Though you lean on some object, do not rely on it. It is careless to rely on things; you must always maintain your own

FIG. 21 a   FIG. 21 b

one point. The same is true in social life. You can be felled by the thing on which you lean or the person on whom you rely.

In all of the Tohei style Ki Exercises we have shown, whatever the movement of the arms and legs, whatever the posture, you can always maintain the one point. Though, at the training hall, we can only practice for a limited amount of time, wherever you are and whatever the time, you can practice maintaining the one point on your own if you decide to do so.

If you practice everyday you will gradually reach the state where maintaining the one point becomes a matter of course, and you will feel bad if you do not maintain it. When you get to this point, *ki* will be constantly emanating from your entire body, you will be healthy, and carelessness will disappear from your daily life.

Because some people think differently on this point, I should like to take this chance to explain in more detail what I mean. Sometimes people ask "If I spend all of my time thinking about maintaining the one point, won't I get to the stage where I cannot think about or do anything else?" This seems reasonable, but the fact is that maintaining the one point and constantly thinking about it are not the same thing. The one point in the lower abdomen is not a tangible point but a point infinitely condensing. If it becomes too small to perceive, just leave it condensing. Once you keep one point, you can maintain it naturally without thinking as long as you keep a correct posture. The weight of all things is in the lowest part, and this point is the natural place for the weight of the upper body to settle. It is only because the action of the mind can upset this arrangement that at the beginning we say you must concentrate your mind in this point and keep your weight settled where it should be. Then you can maintain the coordination of mind and body.

When you have managed to achieve this state, then think about how you feel. It should be a completely natural and at-ease condition. When you understand the feeling, in that condition you can do or think anything you want. On the other hand, if in the meanwhile the condition becomes upset and you recognize that it is upset, you should think to yourself, "It's time to maintain the one point," and get back into the correct state.

When you are angry or startled you will have lost the one point. This is often the case when your shoulders are stiff or you are tired. In all of these instances, it is time to restore yourself to the condition of maintaining the one point.

At first, you may find that though you can maintain the one point, you can also immediately lose it. You may go all day without remembering it a single time, but if you practice diligently, the length of the period in which you can maintain the one point will increase, and you will learn to know the minute you have lost it. When something big is about to happen and you begin to worry, you are likely to make a great flop. But if on a similar occasion you realize the seriousness of the situation but decide that it is time to fix the one point, you will keep a cool head. Soon, you will get to the point where you maintain the one point without noticing it yourself.

A seventy-year old man in Hawaii, who was learning aikido with mind and body coordinated, used to practice with the one point as he drove his car. Of course, thinking of only this while one makes a long trip is not a good idea. This man unconciously concentrated *ki* in the one point just as he saw the accident was about to occur. He was driving along a mountain road when suddenly a truck appeared from around a corner. It was raining, his car slid, and the two vehicles crashed together in a head-on collision. The front of the elderly man's car was crushed. Ordinarily the steering wheel would have smashed into the man's chest, but he was completely unhurt. When he checked, he found that the steering wheel was twisted. At the instant of the crash, he had twisted the wheel with his own hands, though he did not know why or how.

Naturally, because he was maintaining the one point, powerful *ki* was flowing from his body, and his arms had become unbendable. The impact of the collision directed toward his body was diverted to pass through the steering wheel. The old man happily remarked that he had a chance to experiment with the power of *ki* in a moment of peril.

The strength of *ki* when mind and body are united is extraordinary. You can be prepared to manifest this strength at any time if you always maintain the one point. By practicing your one point occasionally in your daily life, you will be able to manifest anytime the power of mind and body coordination which is originally yours and to navigate easily and powerfully in the waves of this life.

EXAMPLE 8
Rowing Exercise

A stands with his left foot one half step forward, with both wrists well bent, and with both hands at about hip level. At the first command, leaving his wrists bent and opening his fingers, A thrusts both hands forward. He simultaneously thrusts his upper body and hips forward, bending his left knee forward and lightly extending his back leg,(*fig. 22 a*).

At the second command, he forms his fists as if he had grabbed something and simultaneously drawing his upper body and hips in, pulls his fists back to the hip position (*fig. 22 b*), bending his right knee slightly and extending his left leg. This exercise, called the rowing exercise, should be repeated many times.

When A is in the position in *fig. 22 a*, B attempts to push both of A's arms toward his shoulders. He may also attempt to push A's knees, back, or head from the rear. If his upper body bends forward or if he tenses his arms, he will lose the one point and will be unstable if pushed.

If A keeps his upper body in the correct position indicated by the dotted line in *fig. 22 a*, and maintains the one point, B may push where he likes, but A will not move. When A is in the posture indicated by the dotted line and must maintain the one point. In this case, though B attempts to lift A by his hands, A will not move because the weight of his upper body is underside. This exercise, in which you move the upper body back and forward and extend and retract your arms, is good practice in maintaining the one point while other parts of the body are in motion. B should make suitable tests of A's stability throughout the exercise. If A is properly maintaining the one point, B will be unable to move him.

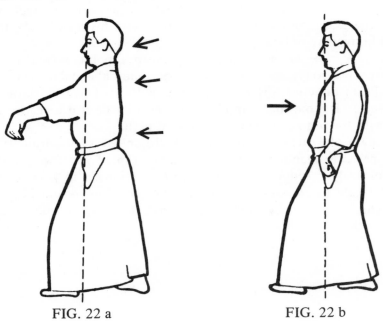

FIG. 22 a   FIG. 22 b

As you extend your arms, *ki* should flow out abundantly from both or you will lose the one point and totter when you are pushed. This is not an arm exercise. It is designed as an exercise for the one point and as an exercise in extending *ki*. Through it you can greatly strengthen your hips.

You must never tense your legs and always move them naturally. Though some people, attempting to do their best, always tense their legs, this makes them weaker. Be careful concerning this point.

EXAMPLE 9
Being Pushed from Behind.

A extends his left foot a half step and assumes the foot position in *fig. 22 a.* B attempts to push A's hips downward, out of position.

I.   If A tenses his legs sufficiently (*fig. 23 a*), B will succeed.

2.   If, on the other hand, A stands comfortably with his legs relaxed and maintains the one point, B will be unable to budge him, (*fig. 23 b*).

From this you can probably see that you are much stronger if you relax.

FIG. 23 a

FIG. 23 b

EXAMPLE 10
Swinging the Arms

A extends his left foot a half step, lets both arms hang by his sides, and forms relaxed fists.

1.   At the first command, he relaxes and extends his fingers and swings his arms upward to eye level, (*fig. 24 a*).

FIG. 24 a   FIG. 24 b

2.   At the second command, he strikes downward with the little-finger side of the hand, that is with what we might call the bottom of the hand, as though he were hitting something. He then forms his fists and brings his arms to his sides,(*fig. 24 b*).

As in the preceding exercise, B should perform tests of A's stability as he goes through this exercise. A must constantly maintain the one point and hold his upper body straight. Though at a glance it might seem that the exercise would be more powerful if we tensed our arms, the reverse is true. If we tense up, our opponent can easily move us anywhere he likes.

Keep the weight of the upper body always in the one point, and keep the upper body central line straight. Working from this line, and using the shoulder joint as the center, and the length of the arm as the radius, move your arms so as to describe a semicircle with your fingertips. If you shorten or extend the length of the radius during the process you will not make a circle. Since *ki* is always flowing out from your fingertips,extend your arms to the fullest and you will generate great centrifugal power.

This arm swing is so natural that you will think at first that it cannot generate to much strength, but it really does. Because you are not tensing your arms their weight is always underside. When you lower your arms, the descent is extremely powerful just as it is in the test shown in *fig. 15 b*. Moreover, since your arms are always unbendable when they are extended, no amount of pushing can bend them back.

Though this is an extremely comfortable arm swing, it is difficult to master. The following method will probably be of help.

1.   Stand naturally, and keep the line of your upper body straight.

2.   Spread the fingers of your left hand, relax your arm and be completely at ease. Without moving your shoulder, quietly and naturally swing your arm forward and back.

3. Gradually increase the amplitude of the arc through which your arm travels until your fingers come to eye level. Since you must not move your shoulder in the descent, stop your hand at your hip, and do not swing it any farther to the rear.

4. When you feel that your left arm is moving with centrifugal force, swing it together with your right arm.

5. Maintain your body's straight center line, and swing both your arms and your hips simultaneously to the front and to the back.

This method should help you to master the swing easily. The movement involved is very important in aikido with mind and body coordinated techniques, and you should practice it thoroughly and often. It is an arm swing in which *ki* is always flowing forth from the arms.

EXAMPLE 11
Changing Directions

A performs steps 1 and 2 in example 10 and then immediately, leaving his feet in place, turns sharply to the rear by rotating his hips to the right. He then awaits the command, (*fig. 25 c*). At the command of 3, he performs the same exercise, (*fig. 25 d*), and at the command of 4, he brings his hands down and turns to the left to resume the position in *fig. 25 b*. When he rotates his hips he must always keep his fists formed at his hips. This amounts to performing the exercise in example 10 keeping both feet in the same position, changing direction, and swinging your arms back and forth in the new direction just as you did in example 10.

A should repeat this exercise to the commands of 1, 2, 3, 4, a number of times. As he calls the commands, B should attempt at the position seen in *figs. 25 a and 25 d* to push A's hips forward. Usually in the first set of exer-

FIG. 25 a   FIG. 25 b

FIG. 25 c

FIG. 25 d

cises, A will remain stable as in *fig 25 a*, but he may totter as in *fig. 25 d* after he has changed directions and is repeating the exercise.

This is because in *fig. 25 a*, A is facing in the original direction and he is maintaining the one point. But after turning all of his *ki* does not flow in the new direction, a part of it remains flowing in the original direction. This means that the *ki* stops flowing from his hands, he loses the one point, and stumbles when B pushes him. None of this would happen if he kept all of his *ki* flowing before him after the turn just as he had been before the turn. As we said earlier, outpouring of *ki* and maintaining the one point are inseparable. If you fail to keep your *ki* flowing always in the direction in which you are facing, you will upset the one point.

This exercise is designed to develop the ability to change spiritual directions as well as to help with the one point. We must not allow our minds to be lazy. We must train ourselves so that we are always able to freely make our minds go in the direction in which we want them to go.

Let us assign the value of 10 to our mind strength. When one is facing A he is using all of his mental strength, or 10; but when he turns to B, if half of his mind remains with A, his mental strength decreases to 5. If he continues to turn to C and D, his mental strength will dwindle to 0. In today's busy world we seem constantly to be having to face things when we have 0 strength. By practicing changing mental directions so that, at an instant, we can transfer our entire mind from one direction to another, we will always have strength of 10 to face whatever comes. No matter how busy we are, we can train ourselves to be able to promptly tackle all of our jobs one by one. Only then can we reach the point where we can manifest the very ultimate of our powers.

Though it is easy to direct your mind to things you like to do, and hard to direct it toward trifling things that you do not like, practice with the one point will help you turn all of your mind even to unpleasant tasks.

Chapter 7 | Tohei Style *Ki* Breathing Methods

There have long been a number of methods for attaining spiritual unification. Unification means power. Just as if we concentrate light rays on a single spot we develop great power, so by concentrating our mind we can give birth to equally great power. The people of old said, "If you want to, you can do anything." People who fulfill important tasks are always those who excel in being able to concentrate their mind. Believing in God and praying with all your heart is certainly one way of unifying the mind. There are many clear historical incidents of people whose true religious faith has given them great strength. Seated quietly with one's eyes closed, as we do in Zen meditation or in yoga, is also an outstanding way of unifying the mind. A scientist wrapped in his work or a farmer intent on his labors are instances of people who have unified their minds.

Many people in this world, however, are unable to concentrate their minds on one thing. Many others, though they manage to concentrate temporarily, are weak in powers of concentration. Just as we might expect, the ability to concentrate requires training.

Right now, I want to introduce Tohei style *ki* breathing methods as a method of spiritual unification that anyone anywhere can practice daily. The number is considerable. In some you inhale through the nose and exhale through the mouth, inhale and exhale through the nose, inhale through the mouth and exhale through the nose, or in others you add some motions as you breathe. Amont them, there is one long known in Japan as misogi breathing. I developed it into a Tohei style *ki* breathing method through applying the principles of mind and body unification. It is not only the method which beginners can most readily learn, it is also the most effective.

I.   THE TOHEI STYLE KI BREATHING METHOD I

1.   Kneel erect with your big toes crossed and with enough space between your knees for two fists. Rest both hands lightly on your thighs. (Note: When you first begin kneeling this way your legs are likely to become tired; but with practice you will become accustomed to the position, and the strength of your waist section will increase tremendously. Although for those who absolutely cannot kneel this way it is all right to sit in a chair, the kneeling position is by far the better.)

FIG. 26a

Hold your upper body erect and stretch your back muscles upward. The weight of your body should be concentrated in the one point.
Relax your shoulders, and be at ease, *(fig. 26 a)*. From the beginning of the exercise to the end keep your eyes closed.

FIG. 26b

FIG. 26c

2. Form your mouth into the position for making the sound "ha". While letting a small sound escape your mouth begin quietly exhaling a long breath. Without stopping, let out as much breath as you can in the direction of the arrow in *fig. 26 b*. We ask you to make a small sound because if you

FIG. 26d   FIG. 26e

do you can conveniently tell if your breath ceases midway and because from
the sound you can tell whether you are exhaling quietly or not. The sound
must be a clear long one. Usually this breath lasts for thirty seconds, but
since this is a little hard on beginners, twenty seconds will be adequate. With
practice you will be able to exhale for a longer time.

3.   When you think you have exhaled enough, incline your upper body
slightly forward and force out one last breath. Even when you think you
have gone about as far as you can, usually there is a little breath left. To
make sure there is no breath left in the body take special care and force
out one last breath. This time the breath will travel in the direction shown
by the arrow in *fig. 26 c.*

Even when you have exhaled all your breath, you must not lose the one
point in the lower abdomen, because if you do you will find it difficult to
inhale in the next step.

4.   When you have completely exhaled, wait a second or two, close your
mouth, and making a small sound begin inhaling keeping the inclined post-
ture. If you inhale directly into the chest you will be unable to inhale fully.
You must always inhale quietly in the direction of the arrow in *fig. 26 d.*
From beginning to end, the inhalation takes about 25 seconds. When you
think you have inhaled all you can, draw in one last breath.

5.   When you inhale in the direction in *fig. 26 d* you will naturally draw
yourself up slightly. Now you must return to the original position so that
your weight is again located in the one point in the lower abdomen *fig. 26 e.*
If you do not keep one point in the lower abdomen it will be too painful for
you to hold it in for ten seconds. The next exhalation will be disturbed. If

you keep one point, you can relax completely. Then you will be able to hold your breath completely, even for thirty seconds if you want.

6. Concentrate your breath on the one point in the lower abdomen, when ten seconds have elapsed, draw yourself up slightly and open your mouth, and quietly begin to exhale.

Repeat this breathing exercise any number of times. Though actually the process of one inhalation and exhalation should take more than a minute, beginners may begin by setting forty seconds as their aim.

Though some people say that when you inhale you should not inhale fully but should hold one eighth of your breath, and others claim that when you have inhaled you should let a little air leak out and then hold your breath, both attitudes indicate ignorance of the one point in the lower abdomen. The idea behind both is that if one inhales fully it will be too painful to bear. Actually, we must learn the painless method in which we inhale completely and to concentrate all of the breath in the one point. If our breathing stops during the process or if it is rough, we have clear indication that the one point is lost. Maintaining that point makes it possible always to both inhale and exhale in long, quiet, even breaths. Making a sound is the best way for beginners to practice on their own because it lets you know immediately when your breathing method is mistaken. When you perform this breathing excercise, remember that it is not merely a matter of inhaling and exhaling. You must approach it with real spiritual concentration.

Breathe out so that your breath travels to heaven; breathe in till the breath reaches your belly. In other words, when you exhale do it so that you feel that your own breath will not expire before your eyes but will travel to the shores of heaven. We say this is *ki o dashite haku* or exhaling as we extend *ki*. In this method though our breathing is quiet it has strength. In inhalation we say we must draw in the *ki* of the universal completely and concentrate it in the one point in the lower abdomen. In other words, we feel as if we were drawing the universal into our own abdomen. When we have exhaled all of our breath, we are in a position of having put everything into the hands of the universal. When we have inhaled completely we are at one with the universal. At first, you may be uncomfortable, your breathing may be disorderly and liable to break off midway, but if you repeat the exercise for ten or twenty minutes, your mind will calm down, and breathing will become comfortable. With constant practice, you will reach the stage where your breathing will be long and calm and comfortable right from the start whenever you decide to perform the exercise. You will by then have forgotten your own body and will have entered into a world of nothing but breathing. You will feel as if it is the universal, not you yourself, who is doing the breathing. Finally you will come to comprehend yourself as a part of the universal. You will not realize the effect of breathing methods overnight; it takes discipline to enter its world.

When you have gotten to the point where you can practice your breathing method successfully in the proper kneeling position, you will be able to practice it anywhere, anytime whether you are standing, sitting in a chair, walking along, or lying down. When practicing while walking calm your mind by concentrating on the one point in the lower abdomen, and walk gently along the surface of the ground. Do not agitate the one point in the lower abdomen. If you shorten both the inhalation and the exhalation time slightly and extend the time in which you support the one point in the lower abdomen you will be able to practice quite comfortably. This is an extremely effective method of calming your mind even as you walk along.

To practice breathing while lying down, lie flat on your back with your legs stretched out straight. Since it is difficult to aim your inhaled air at the back of your head while you are lying down inhale only as much as you can without straining, and concentrate the air in the one point in your lower abdomen. In this case also, shorten inhalation and exhalation times, and lengthen the time you hold in the one point. This method is useful when you are sick.

You can also practice breathing while you are driving or while you are waiting for someone. If you are in a group of people where it would be embarassing to open your mouth and make a sound as you breathe, follow the same general breathing pattern, but inhale and exhale through your nose. In ten minutes' practice you can acquire ten minutes' power, in an hour's practice an hour's power. Even if the practice periods are short, if you use them without waste their effect will add up to a great deal of power. Do not forget, however, that practicing all the time can easily develop into not practicing at all. Things are as easily lost as they are easily acquired.

The best habit to make is about fifteen minutes of practice just before sleeping and fiteen minutes just after getting up in the morning. You will certainly find that your strength will increase and you will be healthier if you give up fifteen minutes of sleep time for the sake of breathing practice. Incidentally, if you have been studying or doing some work that has tired you, you will find that you will feel much better if, instead of taking a walk to rest, you practice breathing for fifteen or twenty minutes.

If on the occasion of some great incident you are agitated and unable to get a single good idea, resolutely practice breathing for about two hours, and you will be able to make up your mind, as new courage surges through you.

Sometimes it is stimulating for a group of like-minded people to get together and practice breathing. A person of irresolute temperament is likely to give up his practice halfway through, but if there is a group to lead him he can carry on successfully. When you practice in groups, of course, it is necessary to select a leader whose instructions everyone must follow. The leader should have something like wooden clappers to make a noise. When he strikes them together, everyone exhales together. When he strikes them a second time, everyone begins to inhale together. One more strike and everyone once again exhales together. Continue this practice for about an hour. Do not gasp for breath between the sounds of the clappers. Even though it may be uncomfortable, stick it out, and follow the leader's instructions.

If you do so you can master proper breathing, but you cannot if you cheat. If your breathing is uncomfortable because somewhere along the line you made a mistake, it is better to make the effort to find that mistake than it is to cheat. Though the leader himself may be able to breathe long and continuously he should not make himself the standard. He should control his breathing by making it more forceful and shorter so that the new members of the group can keep up.

Humans can manage to live for a time without eating, but if breathing stops for even a little while, all is over. Though we breathe unconsciously, whether our breathing is proper or not has a great effect both on the spirit and on the welfare of the body. A healthy person breathes in long strong breaths; a sickly person breathes in short weak ones. A spiritually stable person breathes quietly and evenly, whereas a nerous person breathes at random and in jerks. We can always promote spiritual stability and preserve health by controlling our breathing. In our body, nourishments absorbed through the digestive organs are broken down and burned to supply the energy needed to sustain life. Oxygen is absolutely necessary for this process. If the body cells are richly supplied with oxygen, the transformation of food into energy takes place efficiently. As by-products of this process, waste matters like carbon dioxide are produced. These waste matters must be eliminated immediately.

External breathing or breathing with the lungs describes the process where air from the external environment is inhaled into the lungs, and the carbon dioxide gas in the lungs exhaled. Internal breathing describes the process where oxygen is taken from the lungs by capillary vessels covering the air cells of the lungs into the larger blood vessels, and thence into the capillary vessels supplying the cells of the body with oxygen. In the opposite direction carbon dioxide produced in the cells are absorbed by capillary vessels which flow into larger blood vessels then into the capillary vessels of the lungs where it is exhaled. The important thing is the internal breathing.

Recent medical reports say that 80% of modern diseases are due to nervous problems. Most people get nervous, angry, or worried unnecessarily and tense their bodies. The capillary vessels naturally contact, becoming narrower and impeding the free circulation of blood. Being dependent on the flow of blood to exchange oxygen and carbon dioxide at the cellular level, internal breathing cannot be complete in this state. As a result, our life power or vitality naturally declines leaving us weakened and susceptible to diseases and disorder. Just like it is more important to prevent fire than to extinguish it, it is better to activate the life power than to cure diseases. The method to activate the life power is the Tohei style ki breathing method. By breathing deeply, keeping one point and relaxing completely, all the capillary vessels open and the oxygen is sent to every part of the body. The nourishments are completely metabolized and the life power is manifested. The diseases of the liver, kidney, heart and diabetes and high blood pressure can be cured easily through the manifestation of your own life power. Tohei style *Ki* breathing method is truly an elixir of life. Through setting aside a little time each day for breathing practice may not bring about any visible results, if we continue practice unfailingly we will be able to cultivate an invisible but powerful undercurrent of strength. By and by, we will reach the stage where we are always able to enter the realm of bodily and spiritual unification, where we are capable of amazing displays of power and health.

Plenty of people can see a lofty tree, but few notice the roots. A tree can grow to be lofty only if its roots are firmly planted. Such things as breathing methods are disciplines that form the roots of progress. Use the time and people ordinarily neglect or waste to practice these root disciplines, and you can grow to towering stature.

2. THE TOHEI STYLE *KI* BREATHING METHOD 2

If we only have a short time, there is a breathing method that consists of inhaling and exhaling through the nose.

I. Stand with your legs open about a half step. In this breathing method you may either open or close your eyes.

Spread your fingers, and let your arms hang naturally, (*fig. 27 a*).

FIG. 27a   FIG. 27b

2. Breathe in as if you were drawing in the *ki* of the universal. Then, as if you were pulling in the *ki* of the universal, close the fingers of both hands in order beginning with the little fingers. As you inhale, rise up on your toes. Inhalation should take about five seconds, (*fig. 27 b*).

TOHEI STYLE KI BREATHING METHODS 67

FIG. 27c   FIG. 27d

3. When you have taken in sufficient breath, lower your fists as if you were about to fall on them, tense the one point in the lower abdomen, and lower your heels, (*fig. 27 c*).

In this case it is not as if your *ki* were sinking into the one point in the lower abdomen. It is rather that you are concentrating all of your body's strength there. This will cause you to feel strength surging all through your body.

Remain fixed in this position for about five seconds.

4. Keeping your mouth closed, begin exhaling through your nose as if you were driving out all of your body's strength. Simultaneously, open the fingers of both your hands, and when they are open turn the palms down as if you were pressing on the surface of the earth. Swing both hands in the directions shown by the dotted lines in *fig. 27 d*. When you have finished exhaling, tense the one point in the lower abdomen, and return your hands to the position in which they seem to be pressing downward. This process should take you about ten seconds.

5. When you have completely exhaled immediately open your fingers, face them outward, and return to the position in *fig. 27 a* to begin inhaling again.

Though this breathing method falls short of the former method in deep mind and body unification and in the propagation of real strength, its advantage lies in the brief time it takes under daily circumstances. Three or four times is enough to do it, and because it takes only twenty seconds to go through one exercise, a whole set only requires one minute.

We have a reason for saying that you should tense the one point in the lower abdomen when you do this breathing exercise. When you are shocked, extremely tired, or angry it is difficult to sink your mind into the one point because, we say, under such conditions we cannot locate that point. This breathing method is very effective in such cases. If you tense your lower abdomen without breathing practice, blood will rush upward and you will find it still harder to find the one point, whereas if you do both, your strength will concentrate in the one point. Once you have put strength all over and relaxed you will be able to collect *ki* in that one point. When you are tired this method will quickly restore your strength by helping you reunite the sundered mind and body to give birth to new strength. It is easy to relax completely if you relax after putting strength all over the body. Even when you are not tired and are about to begin some task, practice this breathing method. It will give you confidence to begin and show what real strength you have.

3. THE BREATHING METHOD THAT TRANSCENDS BREATHING

Kneel properly with your eyes either closed or half open and gazing on a spot about two yards in front of you. Inhale and exhale very, very quietly without making a sound. Sink your mind into the one point in your lower abdomen, and you will become unconsicous of the act of breathing. You will then forget yourself, become one with the universal, and enter the realm in which nothing but the universal exists.

Though this explanation sounds very simple, in fact forgetting one's own breathing and entering into the realm of oneness with the universal demands much discipline. But you will be able to grasp it through the *ki* meditation in which you sink your mind on the one point, it becoming infinitely small by half.

All three of the breathing methods we have discussed depend on unifying the mind and the body for proper breathing. Practice breathing everyday, and without being conscious of it your breathing will become correct. Particularly physically feeble or spiritually unstable people should practice breathing regularly because it will help them activate their life powers and build a healthy mind and body.

When we say that a real man can breath with his heel, we do not imply that the heel has any special organ for breathing purposes. We mean that a man who breathes well breathes with his whole body, even the lowest part of it, or the heel. We also say that this is becoming one with the universal and letting the universal do the breathing.

In aikido with mind and body coordinated when many men attack, some people immediately lose control of their breathing. When this happens their body movements become dull. All of this could be cured by serious, intent breathing practice. When the mind and body are in a state of unity, breathing becomes proper. Then you can use your body freely as you will and perform whatever techniques you want.

Chapter 8 | The Divine Spirit

We have already said that our life is a part of the life of the universal, that our basic essence is the *ki* of the universal, that our life and our body are born of the *ki* of the universal, and that they must return to it. If the basic essence of the body is *ki*, so is the basic essence of the spirit.

Ki Development is a discipline that helps us unite the spirit (mind) and the body and become one body with the *ki* of the universal. In other words, the way to union with *ki*. Why, however, is it necessary to unite things that are innately one?

We are given a spirit and a body in order to continue life in this world. The spirit isolates itself from the body and hinders the formation of a whole with it. For this reason, without learning to control the spirit, we are isolated from the universal. When we say "spirit," we mean it in a wider sense than that usually applied to it.

To exist in this world everything, in the wider sense, is given a spirit and a body. A stone has a stone's spirit which protects the stone's form. Air has air's spirit which protects its formlessness, protects its movements, and achieves its mission. Buddhism explains this by saying that all things have the Buddha nature. This spirit of material things is what we call the property of things. Property in itself is the wider meaning spirit.

Humans, in addition to that which we usually call "spirit," also possess this spirit of material things. The nails have their spirit, the hair its spirit, each cell its spirit, and without our being conscious of it, each of these things is fulfilling its own mission. We generally call all of these things together our "body." This body in the wider meaning is spirit.

A tree takes nourishment through the roots and breathes through the leaves. Trees and grass have life and spirits that keep that life going. In general we simply think of this plant spirit as the process of continuing life. In our own bodies, however, without out being conscious of it, our food enters our mouths and our bodies transport it to where it is digested, transform it into plasma, and carry it as nourishment to all parts of the body. this is our "plant spirit."

Animals eat when they are hungry and cry when they want to cry. They act according to the demands of the process of continuing life. We call this the animal spirit, or in humans the basic instincts. Everyone knows that man possesses these basic animal instincts. Man combines all the spirits of things, plants, animals, and the higher element, which we generally refer to as our spirit or our soul.

Basic human instincts are at the same level as the animal spirit. We consider a person who does not live at a higher level than basic instinct inhuman as he lacks the characteristic traits of humanity.

A person whose spirit has gone completely berserk becomes a thing, because in him only the material and the plant spirits are active. He maintains the outward form of humanity but has lost its characterizing traits. Many of today's young people, caring nothing for the trouble they cause others or for the social order, set out willfully to do nothing but satisfy their own desires in their own way. In these people only the material, the plant, and the animal spirits are active. They are, in other words, animalistic humans on a plane no higher than the other animals.

Man is the creater of a society, the maker of a social order. He can tell the difference between good and bad and knows not to do things to others that he would not want done to him. Man's faculty for judging things sets him apart from the other animals. We call this faculty the spirit of reason. Some animals have a degree of reasoning ability. A dog will not forget a human who has treated him kindly, and the ants maintain a fairly highly developed social order, but they lack the human ability to judge themselves in all things. A person who lacks the reasoning spirit, the characterizing feature of humanity, is no better than the animals.

The human reasoning power develops as we grow and advances to a higher plane as we gain education. First our parents or guardians teach us, then our social environment, and later schools, until gradually we grow into genuine human beings. The reasoning power of an individual who remained in the same wild state in which he was born would never develop to any high degree. For instance, there is an actual case of a child born deep in the mountains who lost both his parents. The monkeys suckled and reared him to adulthood. Naturally, he could not understand human speech. His legs grew crooked, and he could climb trees just like the animals with whom he lived. He was afraid of people from the villages and was exactly like a real monkey. It is said that his human judgement and reason were near zero.

As long as today's parents let their children run loose, as long as society ignores the enviornment of its children, and as long as schools continue to give no more than information in their education, it is only to be expected that children will grow up to be like animals, following where their instincts lead. Juvenile deliquency, one of the world's most pressing current problems, calls out for the parents to be conscious of their children, for society to improve their environment, and for the schools to reevaluate their education system and to recognize the need for more education. We can only create a true society if we implant the spirit of reason in our children and teach them to grow to be humans who follow its dictates.

A great problem arises, however, when people think that once their reason has developed everything is all right. If quite a few educators, considered men of high reasoning ability, and people in high social places commit serious errors against reason, we can scarcely blame children who, though knowing what is theoretically wrong, do even worse things.

Sometimes reason loses out to the desires; that is, the animal spirit rules the spirit of reason. After all, reason cannot completely govern the instincts. If reason sometimes wins over the instincts, the instincts will sooner or later have their day. The usual pattern is one of constant struggle between the two with first one and then the other victorious. The very presence in man of reason causes him the anguish of the constant struggle, an anguish unknown to unreasoning beasts. Though some lugubrious folk moan that it would be nice to be like the animals and without thinking at all do exactly as they like, or that they want to be a bird or a shell at the bottom of the sea, others bravely conquer reason with instinct and dare to do as they want.

The fact remains that reason cannot always conquer instinct. Reason is something cultivated after birth; instincts are with us from our first moment. We cannot expect to completely control an innate characteristic by means of an acquired one. If man were born into this world only for the sake of the constant suffering of the battle between reason and instinct, this would be a sorrowful world indeed.

There is, however, no need to worry, because man is endowed with a spirit even finer than that of reason, an innate and fundamental spirit. We are born of the *ki* of the universal and are one with that *ki*. We have a direct connection with the spirit of the universal, and it is this spirit that lets us know that we are one with the universal. This is not a matter of judgment with the reason, it is comprehension with the entire body and soul.

We call the faculty that enables us to comprehend in this fashion our divine soul. Because this soul is directly connected with the universal it has the power to control both the reason and the innate animal instincts. Once this divine soul is clearly manifest reasoning errors cease, and the instincts of themselves no longer run wild.

When, as is sometimes the case, a craven villain turns completely good, it is because the divine soul has opened its eyes, and the man is no longer able even to think of, much less commit, an evil act.

People of deep faith often have spirits of such an almost incredible benevolence and charity that they are gladly willing to forget themselves and devote their bodies and hearts entirely to the good of others or of society. To ordinary people this seems a thing of great pain, something demanding extreme effort in overcoming oneself, when in fact, it is only the manifestation of the divine soul in the real believer. The man of faith is following the commands of that divine soul. Rather than a matter of pain and anguish for him it is one of boundless joy.

A certain virtuous Zen priest once said that every morning when he awakened he asked himself, "Is your master up?" He would then reply to himself, "Yes, he's up." He repeated this from time to time during the day. In Zen, the usual thing is to refer to oneself as *shoga*, or the smaller self, and to our basic essence as *taiga*, or the greater self. Zen also teaches that to discard *shoga* is to give birth to *taiga*. This is the same as admonishing us not to be a slave to our smaller selves but to open our eyes to the basic essence that is one with the universal. The spirit arising from the greater self is the divine soul. By asking if the master is up, the Zen priest was asking himself if his divine soul, his greater self, was active. His calling was a way of making sure that the divine soul always manifests itself. If he felt as if that soul were clouded over he could call it forth by asking, "Is your master up yet?"

The ultimate aim of breathing practice and quiet seated meditation in both Zen and Yoga is a comprehension of our basic essence, which is one with the universal, and a manifestation of the divine soul. Whether we are conscious of it or not, usually a mixture of our material, animal, and reason spirits moves over us like the waves stirred by the wind on the surface of a lake. Just as the reflection of the full moon, shattered into thousands of splinters by the waves on the water fails to give a true impression of the moon, so if the spirit is turbulent it can give no true reflection of the universal. Turbulence can lead finally only to an inability to judge right from wrong and to a reversion to the rule of the instincts.

We must unify our mind and body, calm the waves in the spirit, and make ourselves as a polished mirror in which the true reflection of the universal can clear our judgment and free us from mistaking good for bad. When we do something bad the voice of what we call our conscience tells us that we should not do it. This conscience comes from the divine soul, but when the spirit is turbulent, the voice of conscience is lost in the roar of the waves. When our spirits are calm, however, the voice of conscience thunders with absolute authority. Man is only the lord of creation when he clearly displays his divine soul.

In Ki Society, we constantly train both when quiet and in the midst of motion and activity to unify the mind and body, to be one with the *ki* of the universal, and to keep our spirits as smooth and placid as a polished mirror. This is why we must always be in a state in which we manifest our divine soul, and must always have the strength to judge for ourselves what in this world is good and what is bad.

A man who progresses in the techniques and in becoming strong but fails to grasp the ability to judge good and evil is not a true follower of aikido with mind and body coordinated. A man with an evil element his humanity who becomes stronger in techniques works greater evil, not good, in this world. We must become a sincere man who judges correctly and does right through the practice of *ki* and the manifestation of the divine spirit. To achieve this distant and grand way we must continue to press on by mastering one discipline after another.

Chapter 9 | The Spirit of Love and Protection for All Things

All things change according to the way we look at them. The universal is constantly growing and developing, and the process of death and destruction continuing.

Though the Christians teach that God is Love and the Buddhists that the universal is compassion, quite a few other people hold that the universal is heartless. If we turn our eyes to the creative developing side of the universal it seems to be love, whereas a look at the death and destruction aspect leads us to believe that it is indeed heartless. The universal itself says nothing and leaves the decision to the observers. If we want to create a nasty world and invite a miserable life all we need do is adopt minus *ki*, view everything through it, and define the universal as heartless. When your spirit is negative, whether times are dark or fair, you will always feel haunted by ghosts and demons. Nothing you see or hear will interest you, and you will make no attempt to understand the love of the universal.

On the other side of the coin, if your spirit is positive, whether skies are bright or gray, you will always see them as blue, and everything you see and hear will be pleasing to you. Though it is true that death and destruction exist in this world, the person whose spirit is positive regards even death as priceless. If there is death, birth must be both of great value and abundant. I remember once reading a story about how things would be if there were no death, if people lived for ever.

A man who had an extreme fear of death was granted eternal life. Though, at first, he was overjoyed, he later became bored with human life and tried to kill himself by jumping from a cliff. He did not die. He tried poisons and hanging but was finally forced to realized that death did not exist for him. He also learned that everlasting life is no pleasure, that it holds nothing but the enforced agony of tedium.

We make efforts in our life and find value in our life because death exists. Of course this is no more than a story, but it has some truth in it. Death is a form of love sent by the universal.

We understand the goodness of food when we are hungry and the blessing of good health when we are sick. When the sense of taste is gone, nothing is a feast. When the sense of gratitude and happiness are forgotten, nothing in the world brings gladness. Both lack and want come to us as a form of love from the universal. If you think this way, you can find happiness even in times of deprivation. When you are ill, you can consider it a heaven-granted rest and use the wonderful opportunity you have for training your spirit. When you are well again, you can enjoy the feeling of good health. Nothing in the world will be unpleasant.

If your spirit is positive and grateful for the love it receives from the universal, plus will call plus, and the gods of good fortune will surely smile on your life.

Once we are one with the universal, the reflection of the universal that appears in the divine soul is always in the form of love. It is a manifestation of the spirit that says we must love, protect, and nurture all things. The discipline of *ki* is the refining of love within our own spirits as part of the universal spirit. We do not fight with our opponents to win or to lose. Both men mutually correct each other's weak points, polish each other as whetstones, and mirror each other's actions. Through the spirit of mutual respect and mutual love we train our bodies and spirits till we approach a state of purity and love.

If all peoples have the spirit of love and protection for all things, this world would become a paradise on earth.

PART TWO

Way of Life According
to the Principles of *Ki*

Chapter *10* | Getting Up

Whatever you make up your mind to do, you need a strong will. However valuable the thing you study, if you do not see it through, it will come to nothing. A person of weak will, even though he thinks he is on the right track, will be unable to continue what he begins and will succeed in nothing.

Although many people to whom I teach the one point in the lower abdomen and plus *ki* actually practice what they learn, discipline themselves, and get results, the number who start and stop after two or three days is not small. Complete mastery cannot be expected from only a little effort. You can only succeed in unifying your mind and body and in manifesting the divine soul through ceaseless effort. People who practice for a couple of days and then grumble and criticize *ki* training are only exhibiting their own superficiality. Whatever you begin, you must call forth plus *ki*, maintain a firm will, and see the thing through.

Just as a year has only one New Year's Day, a day has only one moment when you wake up. If you awaken with an unpleasant feeling, without your being conscious of it, that feeling will stick with you, call forth minus *ki*, and make the entire day unpleasant. You will think to yourself, "I woke up this morning feeling heavy, and nothing has gone well all day."

Tohei style Ki Development is a training for a constant outpouring of plus ki, which you must call forth when you get up in the morning. You should get into the habit of coming wide awake, kicking back the covers, and jumping up the minute you awaken. Some people awaken and lie around refusing to get up basically because they are weak-willed. First of all, at times like that, nothing distinct comes into your head, your consciousness is vague, your sense of reason is dulled, and you are in a state of subservience to your instincts. Lying in bed drowsing can help give you the bad habit of letting your instincts get the better of your reasoning. Because sleep is the time when the *ki* of the universal flows into your body, you should sleep soundly, but lying in bed after you have once awakened will not rest your body. You must jump straight out of the bed resolutely because then you will call for the plus *ki* that gets your day off to a positive start. Doing this alone can do a great deal to strengthen your conscious power. Young people who intend to develop themselves, should be particularly careful to cultivate this habit.

When I was young, I was frail both in spirit and in body. Because I slept poorly at night, I was drowsy and heavy in the morning and found it extremely difficult to get up. Whatever I started, my perseverance would give out, and I would give up halfway through. I thought it was all the fault of my bodily weakness.

At sixteen I spent a year in treatment for pleurisy, but the illness got steadily worse. Now, when I think back on it, I realize that I gave into the disease and with completely minus *ki* retarded my own recovery. I spent all my time worrying that maybe even if the sickness passed I would not recover completely, and I got no stronger at all.

In that one year of treatment, on the other hand, I had an opportunity to reflect on myself and see that I could not continue the way I had been going. I read a number of self-improvement books that came my way. These made me realize that I had to do something to temper my own body.

While I was reading one of these books I came to the full realization that my own will power was weak and that I had to discipline and strengthen it. "All right," I said, "Let's work on the will power. This at least is something that I can do." The doctor told me that I still could not exercise, so after a lot of thought, I decided on taking cold baths everyday.

It was summer then, and the cold water was pleasant. Every morning I would leap up as soon as I awakened, run to the bathroom, and dash two or three buckets of cold water over my head and body. Then I would dry off and rub my body thoroughly with a dry towel. After a while, I would come conscious in the morning with the immediate idea of cold water. My head would clear up immediately, and I would say to myself, "Lolling around in this warm bed will do you no good." My bad morning habits completely changed, and I slept like a log at night. Gradually, of course, autumn came. The temperatures dropped, the water got colder, but I never even thought of stopping my training. With no sign of suffering, I continued my cold baths all through the cold weather, and my body grew so much stronger that I felt I could do anything I wanted.

Later, I head of the stern disciplines of *Zen, misogi* breathing and meditation while seated under a waterfall. I trained in them and others diligently until I had mastered them. Then came aikido. The cold water baths were the first opportunity. My *ki* became positive, and plus called forth more plus. I was blessed with a fine aikido teacher, and today I have reached the stage where I am explaining plus *ki* to other people all over the world.

The important thing for young people who plan to start now developing for the future is to awaken in the morning, clear their head of the fantasies that come in the night, leap up, and face the day with the positive attitude that, "I'm going to do my best." The first step at departure leads to a thousand miles of progress. Put this early morning discipline into practice, starting right now.

Chapter *11* | Sleeping

To be wide awake first thing in the morning you must sleep soundly at night, because while you sleep your body's strength is recovering from the work of the day. People who sleep not at all or only lightly and fitfully wake up in the morning with eyelids as heavy as lead and with a fuzzy head. These are the ones who lie in bed till the last minute, neither asleep nor awake.

At night, when we sleep and thus abandon ourselves entirely to the universal, the entire brain is at rest. Then the *ki* of the universal passes through our brains and fills our bodies renewing our strength and making us ready to be wide awake in the morning. If, however, our brains are in turmoil rather than at rest, obstacles due to that block adequate flow of *ki*, and when we waken in the morning, because our supply of *ki* is not high, we cannot get up immediately. This is why a short deep sleep is much more beneficial than a long light one.

We usually say that five things are indispensable to human life: something to wear, something to eat, someplace to live, air, and water. This is true in civilized societies, but in southern uncultivated lands these things are not always essential. In someplaces people can live naked and sleep in the shade of the trees. Food, air, and water, on the other hand, are basically essential whoever you are or wherever you are.

Are these three essentials enough then? No, *ki* too is essential. We receive our supply of *ki* as we sleep. Even if we have the five essential elements, we cannot live without sleep. In other words, people cannot live without *ki*.

If during the day we maintain the one point in the lower abdomen and keep our *ki* in constant active conflux with that of the universal we are in good condition. But if we keep on this way without rest we will exhaust our supply of *ki*, and the absolute amount will become depleted. To replenish our supply we need sleep.

People who maintain an active conflux of *ki* throughout the day, take in *ki* actively at night when they sleep. Likewise, people whose conflux of *ki* in the daytime is sluggish take in *ki* sluggishly at night resulting in their sleeping poorly. The results are such that a person who sleeps like a healthy man has an active *ki* flow and gets healthier and healthier, whereas the sickly person who has a poor *ki* flow gets weaker and weaker.

An extremely large number of ordinary people disparage the need for sleep as a supply source of the *ki* of the universal. They disregard the importance of their sleep time, get an insufficient supply of *ki*, get sick, and ruin their *ki* flow. They then have to use sleeping medicine or they cannot sleep at night. They carelessly are shortening their own lives.

Because a person who learns correct Tohei style Ki Development always maintains the one point in the lower abdomen and keeps up an active ki conflux all during the day, he should put his head to the pillow at night and within from thirty seconds to one minute be sound asleep. Moreover, if you have ten or fifteen free minutes during the day and want to sleep you always can quite soundly. Only by awaking alert, keeping up a constant flow of ki through the day, and replenishing your supply of ki at night can you walk the path of life in brightness and good health.

I once spent a couple of days with a doctor who always took some sort of medicine at night. When I asked him what it was. he said, "Sleeping medicine." I then asked if sleeping medicine was not bad for the body, and he replied that he was well aware of its harmful effects but that without it could not sleep. He also said that he could not stop taking the pills because he had to have his sleep to be ready for work the next day. When he began taking them, one a night was enough, but now he needed two. When I asked him if he would like to try a way of sleeping without the pills, he said that he certainly would. The next day I taught him *ki* principles. I also showed him how the mind moves the body, how much strength one can derive from unification of mind and body, and the essential importance of maintaining the one point in the lower abdomen for mind and body unity. I then said that when he got ready for sleep that night he should just go to bed without taking any medicine. If he lost a night's sleep it would not kill him. I told him that he would sleep when he got sleepy, but that if he did not sleep he could take off work the next day or so and it would do no harm. "Try staying awake all night," I said, "If you get bored lying there doing nothing, practice the one point in the lower abdomen that I taught you today. Ten minutes' practice will give you ten minutes' strength. If you practice all night you can amass a great deal of strength. After all, if you are not going to be able to sleep, you might as well use the time effectively. Just lie on your back with your arms and legs stretched out comfortably, and practice concentrating your mind in the one point in the lower abdomen."

I then told him to pay attention to the following point. People who cannot sleep generally suffer from a condition in which all of the blood rushes to the head. The head gets hot, and the feet and hands cold. Whenever you feel that your pillow is too hot, your blood is accumulating in your head. We can change this with thought. All you need to do is sink your mind in the one point in the lower abdomen and think with all your heart that your blood is flowing from that point to the very toenails of both feet. With thought you can send your blood to your feet and make them as warm as can be. Tomorrow make a test of how much power you can develop by using the one point in the lower abdomen. With this final remark I left him.

When I met him the next day, he said that he had intently practiced what I told him and that at sometime or another he had fallen asleep and slept till seven o'clock. "Ordinarily," he said, "when I take a sleeping pill and fall asleep I wake up around four and, try as I may, cannot go back to sleep, but this morning I slept on till seven, dead to the world." He also happily added that he had not felt so refreshed in a long time. Since he learned how to go to sleep without sleeping pills he has been an enthusiastic *ki* follower.

Pour some water into a tub and stir it up. Now try as hard as you can to calm the water with your hands; you will succeed only in agitating it further. Let it stand undisturbed a while, and it will calm down by itself. The human brain works much the same way. When you think, you set up brain waves. Trying to calm them down by thinking is only a waste. People who cannot sleep and lie awake thinking, "Go to sleep, go to sleep," are creating more turbulence in the brain. It is difficult for them to sleep because, as they try to, they are constantly thinking and upsetting their minds. First they trouble themselves with thoughts like, "If I don't get some sleep, I won't be able to work tomorrow," and then move on to such even more useless reflections, as "He said something nasty about me today," until sleep becomes totally impossible. When your mind is upset, lie completely still, and it will calm down by itself. When it has calmed down sleep will come. The old habit of counting to ten until you fall asleep works on the same principle. You do not have to think about counting to ten, and while you repeat the series mechanically over and over, your mind calms down, and you fall asleep. On the other hand, many people find that this kind of simple trick does not work for them.

First of all, we have to maintain a firm conviction that if we cannot sleep we might as well be awake. Humans cannot live without sleep, and sooner or later it will have to come. Because if you are really sleepy you cannot stay awake, suffering to put yourself to sleep is foolish. When you are awake, exercise sufficiently; and when you go to bed, you will be able to sleep. If you cannot sleep, do not feel that you absolutely must.

The second important consideration is to keep your thoughts concentrated. When they are dispersed like the waters of the sea, if first you turn to one wave, others arise from another quarter in unending succession. If you concentrate your thoughts in the one point in the lower abdomen, when thoughts float into your mind you will be able to ignore them. They will then perish like rootless grass and leave you with a calm spirit ready to sleep.

The third thought is to keep your head cool and your feet warm, because often the body's blood rushes to the head and makes it feel hot and heavy, leaving the feet cold with the result that sleep is difficult. From olden times, people have correctly held that the healthy way is to have a cool head and warm feet. If you follow this advice you will find that you can sleep soundly.

In cases like these, practice shifting your concentration by sinking your *ki* into the one point in the lower abdomen. If you then think with all your mind that the blood is gradually flowing down to the tips of your toes, it will do so, and your feet will become warm and your head cool. This works even on feet so chilled that you cannot warm them by the fire. Remember that even though you shift your conscious thinking if you do not maintain the one point in the lower abdomen, the effect will be slight. If when you try to sleep you cannot because the pillow is too warm, try this method.

This method will work, but do not be in a hurry. If at first you cannot sleep, practice the one point in the lower abdomen to make good use of your time.

We realize, however, that on the eve of some big event worry prevents sleep, even though, as everyone will agree, if we do not take a little time for sleep the body may be unable to go on. If you follow the procedures we just outlined and you still cannot sleep, it is because your blood has collected at your head to the extent that you can no longer find the one point in the lower abdomen. When this happens, take thirty minutes or so and practice *ki* breathing. If you cannot spare that much time , lie down and practice the following.

I.   Lie on your back with your hands and feet comfortably outstretched. Breathe in through your nose, and aim the breath at the pit of your stomach. Concentrate it and your bodily strength in the one point in the lower abdomen. Hold this condition for five seconds, thinking with all your spirit of sending your blood to the tips of your toes.

2.   Maintain your *ki* in the one point in the lower abdomen, but relax your physical strength, and breathe outward through the nose. While you are doing this, keep thinking of sending the blood to your toes. In other words, when you inhale and when you exhale keep you *ki* in the one point, and keep sending your blood downward.

Repeat this several times maintaining the one point and relaxing all of your physical strength. You will be able to keep the one point correctly. Once you have corrected your grip on the one point, you can begin with the practice we mentioned earlier.

If you practice this procedure every night, not only will you be able to sleep well at night, but in the daytime, whatever the noise or whatever big event you face, if you want to sleep you will be able to. You will think much better if, instead of trying to use a tired brain, you take five or ten minutes out to sleep for a while.

Anyone who cannot sleep well will envy the man who saying, "Excuse me a while," can drop off for a brief nap. To be able to sleep whenever you like is a special technique and an important element in good health.

Keeping your *ki* sunk in the one point in the lower abdomen and unifying your mind as you sleep has one more important significance. As you sleep, subconsciously you keep your mind unified so that when you do awaken you spring wide awake. People who sleep lightly awaken sluggish, with their minds in disunity, and loll aimlessly around in the bed. The story goes that once a man of the martial arts immediately awakened and downed a thief who had broken into his house and was about to touch him. He could do this because his mind was in a state of unity even as he slept. It is actually more that though the mind sleeps it is unified and always ready to awaken instantaneously.

Chapter *12* | **The Subconscious**

Discipline is all the more effective if we make good use of sleep, the time when we are receiving our *ki* supply from the universal. We spend about one third of our lives sleeping, and whether we use that time to good effect or not makes a great difference to the kind of lives we lead. Training hall practice is not all of *ki* training. We must be able to practice twenty four hours a day, while we are sleeping, as well as during the waking hours.

Everyone has some kind of habits. We do not need to try to get rid of some habits that may be humorous and do no harm, but we should absolutely break ourselves of those that cause error, trouble, or unpleasantness. Because such habits as easily getting angry, getting tired of things too quickly, melancholia, and ultra conservatism can be great obstacles, we should correct them. It does not pay to be presumptious and defend your habits by saying that you have grown accustomed to them or that, for instance, such and such a thing is impossible to bear without getting angry. It also does not do to be pessimistic and feel that, "Well I'm no good anyway, what does it matter?" If you want to correct bad habits, you can.

Our consciousness, or our usual thinking processes, involves such things as saying, "This is a package of cigarettes." When we see the package of cigarettes, however, within our conscious perception of it are all of the experiences related to cigarettes that we have ever had. For instance, notions of what brand, the price, the number per package, and the taste all enter into the picture. This composite of past experiences is the subconscious. In other words, at the appearance of some object, information concerning it from the subconscious gathers to form the conscious. A person who has never seen or has never heard of cigarettes has no subconscious material about them to draw on, and when he sees them, does not immediately form the concept, "This is a package of cigarettes." He can only say, "Here is something or another that is square," and then form a general concept by observing and touching the package.

A similar phenomenon occurs with words. Each person who hears a given word has on hand a large store of subconscious material concerning it, and this material results in vastly differing interpretations of the word.

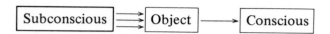

If the conscious is the house, the subconscious is the warehouse in which the building materials are kept. That is, it is the storehouse of the mind where all our knowledge and experience are stored.

Burnt stakes will never become a good house. To build well you must have good materials. Similarly, if you want to create a good conscious, you must have good material stored in your subconscious. If you have only materials for getting angry, whatever you see or hear, you will be so. Consciously telling yourself to calm down will not work because these materials will come to the forefront, and you can do nothing to control yourself. The tendency is to lay the blame somewhere else by saying, "I was born that way," or "I'm no good anyway."

Scolding a child with, "I've already told you about this," when he does something bad is no way to correct him. Though he understands he is wrong, his subconscious will not alter, and he may take the scolding the wrong way. In the end, he may give up, decide he is worthless after all, and go on to do much worse things. Only when the change is complete in the subconscious, can we entirely break ourselves of bad habits.

Many people feel that changing the subconscious itself is impossible either because they do not themselves know a way to change it or because even if they do, they have tried it for a while with no immediate results and have then given up. They then decide that the change is impossible to make oneself or that bad habits cannot be broken.

One drop of clear water added to a cup of tea will change neither its color nor its taste. Two drops will do little more, but if drop by drop we continue to add water, both the color and the flavor will alter. People generally leap to the conclusion that because one or two drops of effort cannot change the subconscious, it is impossible to change it. The truth is that, just as with the cup of tea, if we continue the effort, it will alter.

We all receive suggestions from outside ourselves which influence us. When the weather is fine, we feel fine too, but when the day is cloudy it is easy to be despondent. Praise makes us happy, slander makes us sad. National characteristics differ with the nation. History, customs, manners, climate, and terrain all influence and bring about variations in the people of different lands. All of these variations are the result of exterior suggestion.

In general the color green is relaxing and red exciting. Spanish bulls are not the only creatures whose temper rises at the sight of red. Long ago, to identify a criminal, the authorities would lock all the suspects in a room painted red. The real criminal would see nothing but red wherever he looked. He would have no relief; even when he closed his eyes—red! He would finally go mad.

On the contrary, cities plant trees because of their restful green, and we go into the country because the greenery calms our spirits. Our present sub-conscious is a result of a long period of conscious experiences based on suggestions from all of the things and circumstances around us. Naturally it takes more than a drop or two of effort to change our subconscious content.

Changing your subconscious involves resolving with all your will power from this moment on to embrace only good material. Though up till now, you have been unprepared and have taken in anything just as it was, from now on you must select only the good and reject everything else. The will is man's faculty for selecting and rejecting.

Weak suggestions and powerful suggestions both exist. A weak suggestion may not enter too deeply into our subconscious at first, but if repeated over a long period, it can gain strength. The young man who thinks that, since he is a stable sort, associations with bad companions can do him no harm finds after a while, that evil suggestions repeated often enough bear fruit. He who touches pitch shall be defiled therewith.

A powerful suggestion sinks deep into our subconscious. A fearful fire seen in childhood can become the cause of dreams of conflagrations ten or twelve years later. The fear of fires implanted in the subconscious remains for many years. On the other hand, an evil man who comes in contact with a great man can change completely for the better. Since, doubtless, you can see the powerful action a suggestion has on the subconscious, you will agree that as far as circumstances permit we should shun evil company and seek the close companionship of the great and the good.

Unfortunately, the world is not composed only of people with blessed environments. On the contrary, the greater majority seem to be those who, surrounded by a bad environment, can find no one to trust regardless of where they look. They blame a bad society and a bad environment and consider it only natural that they themselves should go bad.

Whatever the environment, we must build our own personalities. To lay everything at the door of a bad society or a bad environment is tantamount to a statesman who ostensibly is devoted to peace but believes in his heart that all is up with the world. Each person is responsible for himself, and the universal has given each person the means to cope with that responsibility.

The means is *ki* discipline. Always maintain the one point in the lower abdomen, and keep plus *ki* discipline. Always maintain the one point in the lower abdomen, and keep plus *ki* constantly flowing. Then your mind will be too strong for evil suggestions. Though minus *ki* turns everything minus and sinks minus material into the subconscious, plus *ki* makes it possible to change everything to plus and add plus suggestions to the subconscious. If, starting today, you resolve to shun minus elements and put only plus ones into your subconscious, with accumulating effort, drop by drop, you can change your subconscious content. Ultimately, you will manifest the divine spirit, keep your reason, animal spirit, plant spirit, and material spirit subordinate to the divine spirit, reach the realm where, all your bad habits corrected, you will follow the dictates of your spirit, never violating the rules.

Be this as it may, it is only human to be slack or remiss at some time or another, and that is when the unwholesome comes floating along and enters, even if only slightly, into the subconscious. If we do nothing about this evil, it will spread like a summer storm cloud until our entire spirit is blackened. Sometimes just a little something gets under our skins to such an extent that all we can do is fly into a temper. Because this sort of thing affects the subconscious powerfully and, if let alone, will grow like those summer clouds, we must nip it in the bud. It is easy to put an end to this feeling when it is young, but once it has spread, eliminating it requires tremendous effort. When such a thought comes into your head, breathe "Fut" sharply, spit out the thought, and turn immediately to thoughts of plus *ki*.

For instance, if as you are getting ready to go out, you suddenly get the feeling that something bad is going to happen and you leave that feeling to run its course, your *ki* will become more and more negative, and you will be more and more convinced that something bad will happen. Surely enough it will. You can justify the feeling by saying that when you got ready to go out today you felt ill at ease, but it was probably only a premonition. Of course premonitions happen, but in many cases we ourselves invite disaster.

When this happens, breathe out strongly as if to spit out the thought, and immediately stop the flow of it. Tell yourself, "I've got to go out now. I must have confidence, because ample plus *ki* will attract only plus and help me avoid the minus." Change your own *ki* to plus, and eliminate the chance for minus *ki* to creep in. Take particular care that you maintain your plus *ki* because premoitions do happen. We know of a case in which a policeman about to make an arrest, felt ill at ease, changed his *ki* to plus, and miraculously dodged three shots from a criminal's pistol.

In Japan, this has long been famous as the breathing method, a secret technique for ridding oneself of evil. In the case of a man who could do nothing about his quick temper, whenever he felt that he was going to be angry, he would exhale strongly, quickly leave his seat, go out of doors, change his thoughts to positive ones, and return to the room. In this way he overcame his bad habit. Belief gives birth to power. This breathing method requires faith. (If you are in company forceful exhalation sometimes causes embarassment. In such cases, momentarily tensing the one point is also effective.)

We have been talking about practice in taking into the subconscious only good suggestions while we are awake, but methods for doing the same while we sleep are also important, because we cannot afford to permit the intrusion of evil suggestions into the subconscious during the one third of our lives that we spend in sleep.

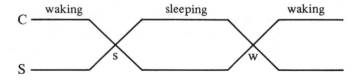

In the chart above, C is the conscious, S the subconscious, s the moment at which one falls asleep, and w the moment at which one awakens.

When a human is awake, C is on the surface, and S is concealed within, but the two criss-cross at point s so that S is on the surface. Dreams are manifestations of the subconscious, manifestations of things that, at one time or another, have gotten into the subconscious. When we awaken, (point w), the two criss-cross again bringing C once more to the surface. Though if C and S completely interchanged at point s, discipline during sleep would be impossible, this is not the case. A part of C remains to work actively together with S. For instance, if during the day a person is almost hit by a car, he will dream over and over of being hit by one. On the evening before an examination a student who is particularly concerned with his work will dream of failing. All of these examples represent the carry over at point s of a powerful suggestion from daytime to a point at which it works together with S. If the suggestion occurs at point s, where one is about to go to sleep, it is even more effective. A man fond of fishing who goes to sleep thinking, "I must get up at three and go catch some fish," even though he is the kind who is usually still asleep at eight or nine, will, without anyone's calling him, be wide awake at three. Long ago, when the Japanese people did not use clocks, if someone had to get up at some particular hour, he would rub his pillow three times asking it to please wake him at such and such a time. He would then wake up when he wanted to because he believed that the pillow would wake him. Of course, their waking was actually the result of their own bedtime suggestion which worked together with their subconscious.

Some people think bad thoughts as they sleep. These thoughts, active in the subconscious, make for bad subconscious material. We should always cleanse our hearts and think only beautiful pleasant thoughts as we sleep. The best way is to practice the breathing methods we mentioned before for 15 or 25 minutes before you sleep. If you maintain the one point in the lower abdomen, and go to sleep with the refreshing positive *ki* of being one with the universal, this feeling will affect your subconscious all night and will be most effective in changing it. If you practice *ki* discipline while sleeping you will awaken on the following morning with an adequate supply of positive *ki*. Naturaliy the sleeping methods we have been discussing are not just sleeping methods, they are also conducive to maintaining the one point in the lower abdomen and to the powerful operation of the subconscious.

If your subconscious material is rich in plus *ki* , the content of your dreams will change. Gone will be the dreams of legs that fail to move, of wolves chasing you, and of suicide over lost love. Instead of minus nightmares, you will have dreams of the attacking wolf, turning and fleeing.

We must remember that when we have negative dreams we will leave behind in the subconscious a great deal of negative material. Bear in mind that regardless of the bold front one presents, if he dreams of cowardice he is sowing the seeds of it in his inner heart. Change all of your *ki* to positive, have only positive dreams, and you will feel good when you awaken.

Since we see that at point *s*, where C and S cross, a part of C continues to work with S, and since we understand that the suggestions given at point s are the most effective, we can make use of this knowledge to correct our own bad habits.

Though of course after we have disciplined ourselves in *ki* training and have progressed to the manifestation of the divine spirit where we can forget about our bad habits because they will vanish, many people still on the road of progress trouble themselves greatly over bad habits. For instance, anyone who gets angry over something trifling and stops his training, can say that he gave up his training for the sake of his bad habits. No reason exists for stopping self training and refining. People who find that they are prone to this kind of thing will find the following discipline useful. It is a method I learned as a young man from my teacher Tempu Nakamura, who himself practiced it at the foot of the Himalaya Mountains, returned to Japan to teach the unity of mind and body for over 60 years, and died at over 90 years of age.

Use a mirror. A small one or a large one will do.

1.   Gaze sincerely at yourself in the mirror for from thirty seconds to one minute.

2.   With strong determination command the face in the mirror to have a mighty will power.

3.   When you have said those few words, go immediately to sleep. You must prepare your spirit to go immediately to sleep without doing anything else.

Since it only takes from thirty seconds to a minute, anyone can do this exercise, but it must be done sincerely and every night without fail.

In number one, you stare in the mirror to concentrate your own will in the self reflected there. You do the exercise sincerely for the sake of a powerful suggestion.

In the second step, merely saying that you really should try to develop a stronger will power is weak. Turn to the face in the mirror and command it to have a mighty will power. Since the decisive command comes both from your real self and from yourself in the mirror, the effect is doubled.

In the third step you only say one thing once, because greedily making a number of suggestions weakens the effect of each and because repeating it two or three times makes the very idea desultory and weak. You go immediately to sleep without doing anything else so that nothing can interefere with the basic suggestion.

Do not expect immediate results from this discipline. Remember what we said about adding clear water, drop by drop, to change the color of a cup of tea. Once you begin this, keep it up every night till you attain your goal. After all, it only takes thirty seconds. You have no reason not to be able to do it.

Though it may take six months to correct a habit, that is not such a long time when you think that you might have been carrying that habit around with you all of your life. Fortunately humans have the gift of adaptability. If you use the kind of suggestions we have been talking about, you will become adapted to them and will be able to accomplish, in five months, three months, or one month, what originally required six. Finally, you will get to the state where results will show up on the following day.

We have only mentioned one suggestion that you can use, but you can try any you like. For instance, if you want to stop smoking and feel that you cannot, simply suggest to yourself that you hate cigarettes. Try as hard as you want, and it is difficult to stop doing something you like, but if in your subconscious you carry the idea that you really hate smoking, or anything else, you can stop doing it with ease. Always use positive suggestions and a decisive command.

In some cases, people put something that makes a person sick to his stomach in whiskey and give it to people who often get drunk and make fools of themselves. The next time that person sees a drink he will feel repulsed. This happens because a violent distaste for whiskey associated with actual physical suffering is deeply carved into the subconscious. You need not go to such an extreme, but you can use the suggestion method to change habits that you would like to break.

A person who stutters has no physical obstruction in his mouth. He stutters because in his subconscious he is convinced that he stutters. When he is as conscious as he can be of it, this subconscious material comes to the surface. Such a person should tell himself not to pay any attention to stuttering. If he ignores it he will be able to converse without stuttering just as freely as he can sing without stuttering. In the case of older children who still wet the bed, it is a good idea to plant in their subconscious the idea that when they want to urinate they will awaken. The child will then wake up when he needs to just as surely as the fisherman gets up early when he wants to go fishing. A child who wets the bed though he is awake is not the victim of a habit, he is a lazy brat.

If you use these various suggestions sincerely, it will take less than six months to correct bad habits. Habits involving the temperament are more difficult to correct and require real earnestness.

Once we understand how much we are affected by suggestions, we must be careful to use only positive words. Without our even knowing it, a carelessly spoken word can enter the subconscious. It is absolutely wrong to say such things as "I'm no good," or "I can't," because this is a way to make yourself no good.

When you must be modest, it is better to use such words as, "I'm immature," because this implies that one will mature and leaves open possibilities for the future. We must also be very careful of what we say to other people because it is unkind to make bad suggestions.

Some parents scold their children by saying, "You've done that again! What a bad child!" If they continue using words like these, the child's subconscious will be completely convinced that he is indeed bad. Once only bad material has collected in the subconscious, the child will really turn bad, and it will be too late to do anything about it. If a scolding is needed, the parent will do better to use words like, "You are naturally a good child so you shouldn't do such a thing. Do not do it again." The idea that he is good and that he should not repeat what he has done will then enter the child's subconscious.

All education should involve changing the student's subconscious. The very idea of attempting to correct the habits of students with words alone when you are unable to correct your own errors is a mistake. The only real way to educate is to first correct your own bad habits, be of strong moral fiber, and have the enthusiasm and kindness to change your students' subconscious. Though it is a different thing if you are only peddling knowledge as an instructor, if real education is your aim, you cannot escape the issue by saying, "After all, teachers are human too." You must make every effort to see that in every word, every sentence, you are imparting a good influence and good suggestions. You must have the zeal to say "If you burn yourself you will become a flame. If you become a flame you can enkindle others. Be moral to teach, be moral to lead."

Teaching demands patience, particularly in the position of a leader in *ki*. However bad the student's memory and whatever bad habits he may have, if he ardently wants to learn, we cannot afford to overlook him. With no facial expression of displeasure and with zeal and kindness, we must repeat and repeat until what we are teaching has penetrated the student's subconscious.

Chapter *13* | The Simple Way

As the world around us grow more and more complex our nervous fatigue gets worse and worse. Large numbers of people are physically and spiritually swept away and exhausted by this complexity whether they attempt to resist or whether they just give in.

Whatever the complications of this world, the universal controls everything in strict accordance with its own rules. If we follow the broad road of the universal we should be able to reach our goal without losing our way in bypaths and side roads. We must not let complications perplex us because we have a very easy and simple road that will keep us going straight.

Recently the number of psychologically ill people has increased. As one doctor said, "An extremely large number of hospital patients today suffer from psychological complaints. Half of the stomach ulcer cases have psychological causes, but since many of the doctors who are supposed to treat these patients suffer from the same illnesses, what can we do?"

Though the basic factors that easily develop into psychological illness are numerous we can divide them roughly into two categories:

I. Lack of control over one's own nervous system.

2. Too much thought given to the complexities of the world and to one's own problems.

The nervous system, passing along the spinal chord to the brain controls the entire body, the internal organs, the skin, etc. It transmits conditions and stimuli to the brain, which in turn gives appropriate instructions to the body in accordance with the stimuli it receives.

If we compare the brain with general staff headquarters, the nerves might be called the messenger delivery service or the information service. If the brain has firm control of these nervous organs, they will all work healthily and correctly. If the brain is upset, command delivery and intelligence will be too, and will seem to act anyway they please.

Let us say, for instance, that the skin receives a stimulus of one. If the nerves convey to the brain that the skin has received a stimuls of one, the report is correct. It is certainly not a faithful report if the nerves report a stimulus of one hundred or one thousand times the strength of the real stimulus.

If you have a fever, someone merely touching your hair will send chills through your body, a slight sound will cause you to start. This is because your nerves are transmitting abnormal information. When you are in a situation filled with complexities, noise, and stimuli, your nerves exaggerate the strength of the stimuli to a point where your brain cannot bear it. When the brain weakens, the nerves become over-sensitive, and the whole viscious circle goes on, leading finally perhaps to a nervous collapse.

In some cases, people have developed cerebral anemia from having a dentist extract a tooth. Because the doctor puts his patients under anesthetic, the pain should not be anything particularly great, but abnormal information from the nervous system causes an abnormal situation. Some people make an uproar over nicking their finger or over some slight incident. A shallow river is constantly turbulent, but it is difficult to make waves on a deep one. A man whose weight is up and whose blood rushes to his head is always in a turmoil. Things do not easily agitate the man who is calm and whose weight is settled.

You can control your nerves correctly if you maintain the one point in the lower abdomen, keep your *ki* outflowing, relax your body, and stay in a natural condition. Maintain in a calm state that says to your nervous system, "Let me know of big things, don't bother me with trifles," and your nerves will not bother your brain with little items like a nicked finger. It is possible to sleep in any noisy place and to have a brain that can select and judge the reports it receives from the five senses and give appropriate commands. A person who is able to do this will never trouble himself over such things as nervous breakdowns.

Now that we understand something of controlling the nervous system, let us turn our attention to the way the brain itself thinks. Simply swallowing up all of the information the brain receives, would in itself lead us to being swept away by the complexities of the world. We must be able to select the necessary information and to discard what is not needed. If we ask ourselves what should we use as a standard of judgement, we see that the real problem is selecting that standard.

That standard is the rules of the universal. If you follow them, you can handle any confusion as decisively as Alexander's sword cut the Gordian knot. This is the simple path on which we can walk through the complicated world. Surely, since we have this road that leads anyone directly and simply to the land of his destination, there is no reason to willfully detour through narrow bypaths. It is good to at last reach one's destination, but the greatest tragedy is to be mistaken in the destination itself, become exhausted, and fall by the way.

We know one universal law: that the mind controls the body. In aikido with mind and body coordinated, when we are going to throw our opponent, we first lead his mind and then send his body to the same place. For this reason, we can easily throw him. There should also be ways to easily handle, through the universal laws, the many things that come to attack us in our daily lives.

Once you have control over your nerves and can easily manage any complication without being bothered by excess annoyances, no changes in this world will surprise you.

Human life is like a man carrying a heavy load on his back and making a journey down a long road. If we add to the already heavy burden we must carry we are inviting nervous collapse. We must cut away all unnecessary baggage and walk triumphantly through this difficult world.

Say we have a drinking glass. Anyone can easily lift it with one hand, but if we were to hold the glass then tensing his arm to the fullest and keeping it so, try to lift it, the glass would seem very heavy and difficult to lift. Though people would laugh at us for making a little glass seem so heavy, in daily life a fair number of people make this kind of blunder. People who make a great fuss over something unimportant or who feel compelled to be angry over nothing are usually making this kind of error and finally reach the point where they cannot move under their own strength. If they would calm down and take another look at the situation, they would find that it is something they could solve quite simply.

Anyone can lift something like a drinking glass because we all know that it is light. But people attempting to lift something heavy often think to themselves, "This weighs a ton," and tense themselves to pick it up. It is a good idea to look back over the things we do. By tensing yourself you are interfering with your own strength and making the thing you are trying to lift seem heavier. When we are lifting a great weight, we should maintain the one point in the lower abdomen, relax, and lift the thing lightly, because this makes lifting heavy things easy. The same exactly is true of matters of this world. When you are facing some grave issue, maintain the one point in the lower abdomen, calm your spirit, and handle the question lightly. If you are tense and worried you become unable to see things, but if you calm down and look clearly at the situation you will always find that there is a way to handle it simply. For instance, when you are driving if you grip the steering wheel with all your might it feels heavy and difficult to move. On the other hand, if you hold it lightly, you can turn it lightly at will. If you worry a great deal about having to make a speech before a large audience, your brain will stop working, your mouth will cease to move, and you will stand like a post on the stage. Under different circumstances, the same person could easily say that the same thing without difficulty. It is the same as standing in front of a single friend and talking naturally, but if he worries and frets about it he cannot do even this simple thing. All one needs to do is to maintain the one point in the lower abdomen and talk as if he were talking with a friend.

If you have some trouble and you turn the thing over in your mind all night long thinking, "If I do this, that will happen, and if I do that it won't work out," you will arrive at no conclusion. You will simply keep going around and around in the same circle, and naturally, no solution will appear. If you run the circuit just once for the sake of argument and find that you come back right where you started, do not waste any more time. Save your strength. Get a good night's sleep and a full supply of *ki*, and when you awaken in the morning you will find you have new ideas to solve any problem.

Since the universal began, for better or worse, everything has a solution. Even things we call unsolvable have solutions. Since things will happen as they must, if we do all we can and remain calm and unmovable in any circumstance we have nothing to fear. Continual grumbling, dissatisfaction, worry, and rushing first here then there are only wasted effort.

Once a young man who had lost his love came to me and said, "I can't forget her. Try as I will, she keeps coming back to my mind, and I can't do anything. What should I do?" When I asked him if he really wanted to forget the girl he said that if he could forget he wanted to. This is a foolish thing to say; if he really wants to forget he should just forget. This young man was wasting his time trying hard to forget because that only made him remember all the more. You cannot forget something as long as you keep remembering it. We tried the forward and backward movement exercise. At the count of three when I pushed his hips, though he had not moved at the first count, he fell over forward. I then taught him the method of switching your mind in which all of your *ki* first flows forward when your arm is outstretched to the front and then to the back when your arm is stretched out behind you. I told him it was no wonder he could do nothing because though he put his arm out behind him his *ki* continued to flow entirely forward. I said that he should practice *ki* for a little while, unify his mind, and practice directing his *ki* in the direction in which he wanted it to go. If he remembered his girl, I told him he should leave the memory be, but practice directing his *ki* to other matters at hand.

In less than a half a month, he was healthy and laughing and his mind was clear again.

If you want to forget something, you should direct yourself entirely to something else. The brain is organized to be able to forget. You reserve all your effort for what you must remember but let the thing you want to forget be, and it will leave your mind. If keep thinking, "I must forget, I must forget," you never will forget.

In all these examples from daily life, whatever the environment, whatever the circumstances, if you calm down, the universal's wide road, along which you can travel easily, is there. Do not give in to your surroundings. The difference between a wise man and a mediocre man is the difference between a man who uses an environment and one who lets his environment use him. Our aim should be to become calm and unmovable, decisive and settled humans. The easiest, the simplest road to follow is the universal's broad highway.

Chapter *14* | **Eating**

All things have life. We are brothers with all things, for all things are born together of the *ki* of one universal. For this reason the all-loving heart of the universal is our heart. The fact remains, however, that we live by making sacrifices of other living things. When we eat meat or vegetables we are taking life so that our life may continue.

How can we resolve the contradiction of saying to ourselves that we must love all things and finding ourselves in the position where we cannot live without sacrificing other lives? Buddhism teaches that killing is wrong to the point where it is forbidden to take the life of an animal or even of an insect. In olden days, a Buddhist could not eat so much as a slice of meat.

Life exists, however, not in animals alone, but in each tree, each blade of grass. Why should it be wrong to kill an animal, but not wrong to crush and take the life of plants? In the eyes of the universal all are equal.

The Japanese have always been a people who love festivals, who love getting together in large groups, drinking, and making an uproar. The real meaning of the festivals, of course, lies elsewhere, but somewhere along the way it has gotten lost, and only the drinking and the shouting remain. The real significance can be found in such festivals as that of the five grains celebrated by the people who have harvested the rice and beans, or in the weavers festival, or in the fish festival celebrated by the fishermen. Knowing that by sacrificing living things they themselves can go on living, people of all occupations hold festivals to raise thanks to the lives they must take.

Though some people believe that man, the lord of creation, is privileged to do as he pleases, the universal must surely eye this as self-complacency.

Though we feel it is all right to call an animal who devours human beings a fierce killer, from the animals' viewpoint how much fiercer is man himself! What then must man seem to the birds and rabbits and grass of the field who can offer no resistance to what he does?

The universal permits us to go on living and sacrificing other lives. We must always be conscious of the significance of this. It is not enough to attempt to console those spirits by offering our thanks. As we said at the beginning of this book, we must always be aware that we, as participants in the governance of the universal, must cooperate with its constant development as the being chosen to represent all other living things. We should not make sacrifices of other things merely to satisfy our own selfish desires.

Other living things have a meaningful existence only when we give thanks to these other lives and let them participate with us in the government of the universal. Whatever plants or flesh we eat we must take gratefully with the spirit, that the lives that have gone to nourish our bodies are not wasted but, by becoming our flesh and blood, continue to participate with us in the work of the universal.

When someone brings your luggage to you from a distant places, if you thank him from your heart and do what you can to entertain him, he will forget all of the trouble the trip cost him and be glad. If, however, you snap, "What kind of a worthless person are you to be bringing this thing around here now!" all his pains will go for nothing. He will grow suddenly tired and resent you very much.

The same is true of the food we eat. If someone has prepared a meal carefully for you and you complain, "Who could eat mess like this?" that person will be greatly disappointed and will harbor a grudge in his heart. The whole situation will end unpleasantly. If, on the other hand, you say, "Thank you for fixing this; it looks delicious," you compensate the cook for his labor and make him happy. How much truer then is this of the vegetables and animals we eat. Until that point, they had been for a long time fulfilling their own mission. Suddenly, they are sacrificed and supplied to humans. If we comment that the things we are about to eat are too unpleasant to be edible, those beings are surely going to flare up in anger and hold ill will against us. If we speak badly of them, there is no reason why they should become our blood, our flesh, or our nourishment. Many people who live on gourmet delicacies are poorly nourished. Before they see the doctor about it, they might do well to examine their own spiritual attitude. These sacrificed lives can only gladly become our flesh and blood when we are grateful and express our gratitude.

We have no right to complain of whether foods are good or bad or whether we like them or not. All of them come from the universal, and we must eat them all as if they were delicious. The very idea of tastelessness, in the first place, is only selfishness. If you are really hungry, anything tastes good. If you think some dish is not good, let your belly go empty until it does look good to you. Do not attempt to put the responsibility for your own body on the food you eat. If you realize that everything has its own taste and are grateful for the sacrifices of the lives that make your food and if you eat everything in this frame of mind, everything will taste good to you.

Because I was bodily weak when I was young, I had a lot of likes and dislikes, but after a long period of training my enlightenment about the way of the universal made me deeply ashamed of my former disliking of things. Since then, for forty years, I have not once complained about food. Since everything tastes good to me, I have no need to complain. Even during the war when we sometimes ate and sometimes did not, I did not complain, and I was not undernourished. Whatever land I visit, whatever I eat, everything tastes good to me.

Once during a meal as I began to eat I was asked how a certain dish tasted. I said, '"It's very good, but perhaps it could be even better with a little more salt." The fact was salt had not been put in it. We had a good laugh over the incident.

The point of the story is, that since I eat everything with a sense of gratitude, the first thing that comes into my mouth when I eat is to say that the food is good. The cook too, who prepares meals from the sacrificed lives of other beings, should exert every effort to make those meals as delicious as possible. Only when he realizes this real significance of his work can a person make progress in preparing foods.

Table manners change from country to country, but manners of the spirit do not. Eat with a heart full of gratitude. A family gathered together having a meal with grateful hearts is the secret to domestic peace. This same spirit can do much to promote world peace. In making a meal we must do all we can to see that the lives sacrificed for it are not wasted, that in keeping with their hopes, we exert our every effort to push forward the constant growth and development of the universal.

Chapter *15* | OurFaces, Our Eyes, and the Way We Speak

Since the mind controls the body, anything that floats, even momentarily, into the mind has an effect on the body. Things we habor for a long time in our minds inevitably show up in our faces, our eyes, and the way we speak.

We are born with our faces. In one hundred people, no two will be exactly alike. If some people are born with beautiful faces, others must be born with ugly ones. Although many people think that we can do nothing about the faces we have always had, in fact they are constantly in a state of gradual slight change.

Today it is possible to alter the appearance of one's face with advanced cosmetics and plastic surgery, but changes of this sort are only temporary. We cannot keep the deception up for very long. Without doing such unnatural things we can change our appearance through the content of our minds.

Look for a while at portraits of people whose names are outstanding in the world, whether they be muscians, scholars, or whatever. If we examine their pictures carefully, we see that though in some cases the faces were not so fine when the people were young, they gradually became splendid. Conversely, compare the picture of some handsome young man with the photograph of the same man taken just before he faced execution for a life of serious crime, and you will hardly be able to believe the two faces belong to the same person.

The spiritual state can change the face completely. Though changing it for the worse is outside our present discussion, we should be embarrassed if we retain the same face with which we were born because this lack of change is proof of a lack of spiritual progress. Only when we have changed our face into something really fine can we say we are a person who has truly grown.

Just as a person, beautiful in his youth, must not settle into conceited negligence, so a person not beautiful should not be despondent because both can work changes on their faces through their spiritual attitudes. This is the no cosmetic method; it is the way to real beauty.

People have always said that the eyes are the windows of the heart because the spirit's condition is most clearly reflected in them. Spirits of love, cruelty, tolerance, or resentment all appear in the eyes.

Since the heart of a man practicing *ki* should be filled with the spirit of love and protection for all thigs, his spirit should naturally be one of love and benevolence. In addition, because his spirit is always unified and is constantly pouring forth *ki*, his eyes will have a latent energy, not a sharp hard gleam, but a light that, together with *ki*, emanates from the very depth of his spirit. This is not the glitter of the thief's eye always seeking the unwary, it is a light that says, "At a laugh, children draw near, but at a frown, wild animals flee." We all need such benevolent powerful eyes.

Among men studying the martial arts, as we might think, some have cruel, savage, and haughty eyes. These eyes, for crushing other people, are not the true eyes of a follower of the martial arts. When eyes like these encounter the true eyes they lose their power to crush. In Japanese, we write the word *budo* (the martial way) with a character *bu* made up of two parts which taken together mean to cease using arms. For this reason the true follower of the martial way must have eyes benevolent enough to do away with the opponent's spirit to fight. However sharp the gleam in your eye with which you try to oppress your opponent is, it will have no effect on him. He will not take it in, it will only return to frighten you yourself. People with hard eyes must understand them as a sign of spiritual immaturity and must strive to discipline themselves in the right way. From time to time, in our effort to progress spiritually, we should look in the mirror, not to see how we look or just to shave, but to judge our spiritual condition. We should seek out the bad places and reflect that, "Here is a place where my spirit is still immature."

Our words, too, are expressions of our spirit. Some people, though skilled in discussions and in receiving and talking to others, create a feeling of untrustworthiness. The old saying goes that there are few good people among those who talk well. Regardless of how clever a man's conversation, if his spirit lacks sincerity he will not attract the hearts of others. The most important element in conversation is to be sincere and to speak from the heart. Only with this as a basis can you make progress in conversational techniques. The kindest words sound empty when they lack love. A person with a dagger thrusts it into his listener's heart with every word and every phrase. When an angry person tells us something, though his words are the most ordinary, his anger is transferred to us. Conversely, a heart filled with love brings untold comfort and strength to others. You need no words, you can communicate to your companion's heart even in silence.

If someone should angrily say to you, "I was only being careful for your sake," or "Even if I say these kind things to you, do you still refuse to understand the way I feel?" before you retort, examine your own heart to be sure you are sincere. If you have love, even if you scold someone, that love will somehow get through to him.

I once served on the board of education of my home village where we had a young man, in charge of sixth-grade boys, who was a most enthusiastic teacher but who often beat his pupils. Before the war, this caused no problems, but afterwards, with the advent of democratic education, the beatings raised a furor among the parents and guardians who began to agitate for the teacher's dismissal. Shortly after I learned of the trouble, I went to see the young teacher. He, imagining that I had come to reprimand him, seemed ready. I first listened to what he had to say.

"This postwar democratic education is good. I agree with it, but the children and the parents have got it all wrong. They misunderstand it, thinking it means non-interference. When the children get a little bit older , they seem inevitably to grow bad. They won't listen to what anyone tells them. If we leave things this way they'll never amount to anything. I know it's no good to beat students, but I go on doing it for the students' sake. I have faith in education, but if you think what I am doing is wrong, I will resign anytime." This high spirited young man said his piece resolutely without giving an inch, but I could sense his quick temper. I had yet said nothing, but he was already getting violent.

"I see," I replied, "I am in full agreement. If you beat your students to improve them, beat them good. I will do what little I can to cooperate and be your ally." The young man was astonished. Of course, what he said was true. The sudden democratization of education brought out certain abuses of privilege. I added to my comments, however, the following remark.

"It is a fine thing that you want to improve your students because you are fond of them, and I suppose, since this is the case, you can beat them just as well when you are not angry. From now on, when you feel that a child needs a beating, check to make sure that you yourself are not angry. If you aren't then go ahead. If you strike them in anger, your own anger, mixed with the punishment, is transferred to the children and will do them no good at all. If you punish them with love in your heart and for their own good, you should be able to do it when you are calm. The students will then understand that you are punishing them with love."

He understood and from that moment never beat another student. If he were about to strike a youngster he would calm himself listen to what the boy had to say, and the necessity for a beating would vanish.

Hear what a man says, look into his eyes, and he can hide nothing from you. If you calm your heart, examine yourself, and look at other people you will be able to understand them. On the other hand, understanding too much is not good. Too much discernment is destructive. That is to say, if you understand a person too well, he is likely to feel cramped in your company and avoid you. If you understand too well, it is also easy to injure others. A father with an eye that is too penetrating oppresses his children, who grow to want to run away. No one likes the glance that pierces the depths of the soul. Just as we keep covered a blade that cuts well, so if we have a strength we should keep it veiled. Though we have brilliance in our eyes we need not dazzle others with it. If we have that brilliance, we should cover it as if it were not there. A wise hawk hides his talons, and a good mouser does not show her claws. It is important to conceal one's own power, because boasting of it destroys it.

If you crow over one of your own good points, you will surely fail in that very point. Use your power only when it is needed, and do not brag. Be just like everyone else under ordinary conditions, but during crises use all of your knowledge and ability. The saying that the sage should be like the fool and the saint like the ordinary man reflects this same situation. If you have modesty in your heart, it will appear of itself in your eyes.

If you have a compassionate heart that lets you laugh wholeheartedly at someone's unfunny joke, or that is reflected in the look of a father watching his children at play, or in the gaze of an innocent lover recalling his sweetheart, your eyes will be gentle. People of this sort do not think ill of being deceived. Though deception makes anyone angry, if we are aware that deception is taking place, we do not lose our tempers over it. It is good then to finally give the deceiver proper guidance and to lead him on the right way. Anyone can bear his naked soul before a person with a compassionate spirit. Leading others is difficult if we are stern.

We frequently encounter people who in a conversation do not look at the person with whom they are speaking but keep their eyes cast down restlessly. Such people are not calm, they harbor some uneasiness. We must learn to be able to look directly at our conversation partner. Conversely, people with the habit of staring directly at other people should make every effort to stop. Wanting to pry into the hearts of others is a childish attitude, not one becoming a disciplined adult. If your spirit is clear, without staring, his heart will be reflected in the mirror of your spirit.

If involuntarily you cannot look a person in the eyes as you speak to him, look at the area around his nose, and he will recognize that you are properly turned toward him.

Though enthusiastic practice, progress in the techniques, and growing strength in aikido with mind and body coordinated are important, they are not enough. You must master the spirit of *ki*. You must learn to be gentle and at ease with others and to have kind eyes and a voice of love that somehow or another hints at possibilities of great liveliness.

Chapter *16* | The Principle of Non-Dissension

All aikido with mind and body coordinated techniques which are based on *ki* principles, begin and end in the principle of non-dissension.

The universal is absolute, with which we have no cause to fight. Battles arise first when the idea of duality appears. They clothe the universal in the light of such dualistic concepts as activity and calm, fusion and disintegration, tension and slackness, and union and separation. By being captivated by the dual world, we have lapsed into the attitude that fighting is the natural thing, that this is indeed a world of jungle law. We have forgotten the true form of the universal, and we will only be able to find it again when we have crossed into the realm of the absolute. The true basic spirit of the universal is the principle of non-dissension.

Because people today find this a very difficult thing to understand, we must actually manifest it through real aikido with mind and body coordinated techniques. A person who has really practiced it has learned through experiences involving his own body how correct and how powerful this principle is. Though, at first, even with practice, the bigger and stronger man has the advantage, this does not mean that the principle of non-dissension is mistaken. It simply indicates that the person losing is not yet equal to the principle; he is still immature. Once a person has penetrated to the real meaning of the principle, strength and body size cease to matter.

As an example, strength and size are important if, when an opponent attacks, you receive the strength of the blow in a collision-like situation. If, however, you brush the blow aside, the opponent must himself manage the force he has generated. If you strain to try to throw some disagreeable person, a fight is sure to start, but since the mind controls the body, if you move his mind to a point you have chosen, his body will gladly follow where his own mind leads. After all, in a case like this, you are actually making him go where he wants to go and turn in the direction in which he wants to turn.

We can avoid quarrels even when an opponent attacks. We must be able to remain peaceful in our daily lives and under any circumstances, and in all places avoid arousing the idea of battle in our hearts.

There are too many people today who feel it is impossible to live without fighting. There are also many who, though it means oppressing others, will stop at nothing to gain ascendency and to win by any means. Naturally, the situation is difficult if these are the people who get together to discuss world peace and concord. The only way to attain peace and agreement among men is for each individidual to return to the basic spirit of the universal and understand the meaning of the principle of non-dissension.

The general belief is that the principle of non-dissension means that we must agree with whatever anyone might say, that we are not to resist if someone should strike us, and that it is very weak and lily-livered. This is really not the case. The principle of non-dissension demands the strongest spirit and a complete supply of plus *ki* in body and spirit to help us avoid receiving even a little of our opponent's mistaken *ki*.

The situation is something like that of a clear spring bubbling from the bottom of a pond so that on its way to the surface not one drop of the pond's sullied water enters the clean stream. When you are filled with plus *ki* and are emitting it, none of the *ki* of people around you can enter your body. Just as the foul waters of the pond would rush in and obliterate the clear water should the spring stop flowing for even a moment, so to if you draw in your own *ki* even a little, the *ki* of all of the people around you will simultaneously attack. The principle of non-dissension demands a strong spirit constantly filled with *ki* and constantly radiating *ki* back to the universal, a spirit whose *ki* is in perfect conflux with that of the universal.

The way of non-dissension enables you to overcome any reversals without spiritual pain, to laugh off any slander, and to lead astray any attack, without yourself receiving the blow.

Those who cry themselves to sleep resisting nothing and replying to no ill remarks made by others, feeling secure that they are not fighting back are not a part of what we mean by the principle of non-dissension.

Locking up the speech and actions of your opponent in your heart is not real non-dissension; it is endurance. Though you say nothing with your lips, your feelings may be seething within you. This, too, is a sort of battle. The non-dissension we are speaking of arises when we do not harbor feelings against our opponent, but with the magnanimity of the sea that accepts all tributary streams, maintain a waveless calm in our own hearts.

An employee of a certain company began studying aikido with mind and body coordinated and came to me one day with a problem. He said that he was frequently having conflicts of opinion with his boss at the office and that the differences would usually end in a quarrel. He also said that his boss was stubborn and that he himself was short tempered. Though he knew fighting was no good he couldn't seem to stop. Whenever someone said something bad to him he always got angry. He wanted to know what he could do to solve his problem. I asked him if he had mastered the principle of non-dissension, and he said that he had.

"It's really quite easy, then," I said. "When someone says something unpleasant about you, maintain the one point in the lower abdomen, send forth powerful *ki*, and do not take personally what he says. If you do this, all of the bad things the other man says will revert to him. For instance, if your boss calls you a fool and you refuse to take in what he says, it returns to the sender, who is in effect saying that he himself is a fool. You would laugh and agree if your boss were to say to you, 'I am a fool,' wouldn't you? Just try thinking this way, and watch the other man's face. The face of a man who is as angry as can be, all by himself, becomes immediately rather amusing."

My student apparently immediately put my advice to practice. However angry his boss would get, he would simply smile and say, "Yes, yes," until finally the boss announced, as he stormed out, that talking to my student only made him angrier.

One realizes when he sees his partner's smiling face how foolish and worthless being angry alone is. The same is true with a threat. If the person threatened simply laughs it off, the one to become frightened is the man who made the threat.

After two or three days, my student's boss came to him and said, "Something's funny here. You seem to have learned something different lately." My student then explained the entire thing to his boss, who said that having quarrels was so much nonsense and resolved to stop.

Often after a quarrel between friends, both say to themselves, "He was wrong, so he has to apologize first. I won't." We say that there is justice even among thieves, and in the case of a quarrel, both are right and both are wrong. If both people are right, there is no reason to fight.

We must consider losing our temper and having a quarrel, regardless of reasons, shameful, but once it has happened there is nothing to do about it but immediately regain the one point in the lower abdomen, calm your *ki*, remove the limits of your generosity, and become aware of your own bad points. It is easy to see the faults of others, but not so easy to see our own, particularly when the blood has rushed to our heads. At times like this, we do not even attempt to see our own failings, but quarrel in a way to mutually point out each other's failings. If we were to examine just where we ourselves have gone wrong, there would be no fight. For this reason when a fight seems imminent, examine your own faults ahead of time, and apologize to your opponent before a quarrel can get started. At least be prepared beforehand to forgive your companion, and you will advance one level higher than he. Fights occur because both parties are on the same level. In the case of mother and child, the mother always forgives because she is on a higher plane than the child. No quarrels occur between them. First take your companion to your heart and forgive him beforehand, and he himself will become confused and realize his own bad points. He will be ashamed to be one level lower than you.

If you have once understood the value of apology, do not let yourself be carried to the ridiculous extreme of getting into quarrels over the right to say you are wrong. The short cut to a solution of the problem is to be broad minded and tolerant of your companion before any fight ever starts. Since it takes two to fight, if you will not be a part of it, no quarrel can take place.

Some people like to tell battle stories but I always reprimand them by asking them how they got into the state where they had to tell such tales.

I ask them if they had nothing else to do before that.

An old warrior code said that three ways to win include: 1. winning after fighting, 2. fighting after winning, and 3. winning without fighting. The first way is the general one and is the lowest level of the three. The second method, which involves complete preparation of all the conditions needed to win beforehand, is safe and is on an intermediate level between the other two. The finest of the three, winning without fighting, is the safest of the three since insofar as no fight takes place no possibility of losing exists. In this method we force the opponent to submit and make him follow where we lead. Aikido with mind and body coordinated follows this path. If we are going to win, we should win in the best possible way. It is exactly because we have no cause to choose the most inferior winning method, that is winning after fighting, that I always reprimand people who like to recount tales of their battles.

It is permissible to use aikido with mind and body coordinated techniques in the following three situations:
1. when your own life is in danger,
2. when another person encounters some danger,
3. when one or two people disturb the majority.

The first case is a pure instance of self-defense making the use of proper techniques imperative. The second involves a duty which it is cowardly to shirk. The third case involves a situation in which no one else can put down the trouble makers so we must use our techniques for the sake of the majority or of society. We are not saying that it is all right in these cases always to employ aikido with mind and body coordinated techniques. We are merely saying that when we have thought out all other peaceful methods of solving the situation and nothing seems to work, then we can apply our techniques.

I remember a case of a young couple who constantly fought and who were on the verge of separation. Since the husband was studying *ki*, his friends came to me and asked me to do something.

Listening to what both sides had to say I discovered that neither the wife nor the husband mentioned his own faults but complained only about the other party. The wife was by no means ready to give in; she gave her husband back three words for his every one. Nothing is as difficult as mediating between a quarrelling couple. Nothing one says will convince the other one. If the mediator says the wrong thing, when the couple patch up their differences, they will direct their ill comments at him. Nevertheless, I made my decision and told the husband that I thought he was wrong, much to his dissatisfaction and his wife's elation.

I said that since his wife was not practicing *ki* she knew nothing about the one point in the lower abdomen and could not help getting angry. He, on the other hand, was learning *ki* and was wrong not to put to actual practice what he learned. I said to him, "If you realize that, whatever happens, whatever your wife says to you, this is the time to practice keeping the one point. Not only will you keep your temper, you will also make a great deal of progress. If you practice the one point only at the training hall and lose it when you get home, you have wasted your effort." I asked him if he would try to do as I suggested no matter what caused the fight. He finally agreed to try it from that day.

I then explained some things to his wife, tried some experiments with her, and got her to master the one point in the lower abdomen. I said, "I realize that you are dissatisfied with your husband on a number of counts, but, as you see, he is willing to make every effort to change his ways. He lacks experience and he may forget, but won't you help him correct his bad habits?" The wife consented, and in less than a month the pair were leading a perfectly happy married life.

When a young couple gets together because they are in love everything should go along nicely, but a single dissatisfaction, on the basis of the theory that minus calls forth minus, breeds further ill until the situation is irreparable.

Instead of thinking to himself at the end of a day's work, "I've got to go home now and listen to her complain," the young husband went home, stopped at the door to make sure of the one point in the lower abdomen, and went in calling out happily, "I'm home." The wife realizing that this was the time to cooperate would rush to the door smiling and saying, "I'm glad you are back." If after she gave her husband something to drink she had something to say she would try to be patient and wait, but if she just could not be still, she said her piece as pleasantly as possible. The husband felt better, always spoke gently to his wife, and became willing to help her with her work. Their love flowed forth, they mutually changed their *ki* to positive, before they knew it, they were once again as close as when they were newlyweds. Later, the wife also took up *ki* training to keep her marital relations on an even keel. Winning and losing are beside the point in married life where the partners must mutually understand and help each other to keep things happy between them.

Though this example is merely one from ordinary life, it points out the need to always remember that there is a way to avoid fighting. There is always a way of coexistence and coprosperity. If we have fighting in our hearts, we make enemies of allies. If fighting is not in our hearts we have neither foes nor allies because all of us are brothers born of the *ki* of the universal. Training in and thoroughly grasping the meaning of the principle of non-dissension is vitally important.

Though the usual sports receive encouragement, technical progress, and popularity from matches of one sort or another, matches are not permitted in aikido with mind and body coordinated because, unlike sports aikido walks the way of the universal and has as its sole aim the perfection of mankind. Perhaps we should explain why matches are forbidden in it.

In the first place, aikido with mind and body coordinated is a discipline designed to penetrate to the inner meaning of the principle of non-dissension. In matches, someone must win, and winning in itself implies a heart filled with fighting. If you strive with all your might to win, it is doubtless very good for you as a sportsman, but with the burning desire to be victorious you may develop the psychology that any means is all right if it helps you win. This attitude can do great harm to you as a person.

Since the true aikido with mind and body coordinated techniques are based on a thorough understanding of the theory of non-dissension, if you fail to grasp the theory, you will be unable to master the techniques. For this reason matches are forbidden. A person who likes contests and matches, should try having one with himself. For instance, a quick tempered man might say, "Today I'm not going to get angry once." If he manages to hold his temper all day, he wins; if he does not, he loses. If we make progress without causing any one else trouble and without bearing ill will against anyone we will get to the point where we are always winning. That is real victory. If we fail to win over ourselves, even though we win over others, we are doing nothing but satisfying our own conceit and vanity. If, on the other hand, we do win over ourselves, we have no need to win over any other person. People will follow happily where we lead. A relative victory is fragile, but a victory over oneself is absolute.

The second reason is applicable to many other situations, but in connection with aikido with mind and body coordinated, it is particularly important that we warn against conceit. Once the conceited attitude arises the door to true understanding is closed. A man who says, "That's good enough for me," has lost the will to learn and master more things. To say to the universal, "I've gone about as far as I need to," is to go against the nature of things. Once we have embarked on the path of the universal, it becomes deeper and wider. An immature person who carelessly permits himself to engage in contests in which he wins soon becomes triumphantly elated and complacent. On the other hand, seen with the eyes of the universal, such personal victories and defeats are no more than a single ripple on the surface of the great sea. The important thing is to cast such trifles from your heart, face the universal, and exert all your might toward self-perfection.

All sports and martial arts matches require rules, particularly the martial arts where sometimes life is in danger. The original aim of sports is to hold a contest of skills in accordance with rules and to enjoy the actual winning and losing. This is perfectly fine in these cases and in those martial arts that are describable as sports. The purpose of a real martial art, however, is quite different in that in both attack and defense we must always presuppose a genuine danger. Whatever the opponent may do, it is useless to complain. We simply must act accordingly. Since our very lives are in danger, we must be prepared in both mind and body.

If we always practice in accordance with set rules, without our being aware of it, these rules sink into our subconscious and emerge when we confront a real moment of danger. We can unwittingly be defeated if we depend on rules that no attacker will follow. One story relates how a young man who always grabbed his opponent's sleeve when he practiced did the same when someone actually attacked him. At the moment when he did so his opponent ripped his stomach open with a knife. Of course we must always take into consideration the possibility that in a real situation our opponent may attack with a knife. Habits we have formed will come out in real situations.

In aikido with mind and body coordinated we think of the many ways an opponent might attack and over and over again practice how we should handle such attacks following the principles of the universal. We sink this into our subconscious and train ourselves so that, even in a surprise attack, we unconsciously act and move the way we should.

If you maintain the one point in the lower abdomen and unify your mind and body like the calm surface of a lake that reflects first the moon, then a flying bird but holds no trace of them when they have passed and yet is ready to catch the lightest blowing of the wind, so to will you not only be able to quickly catch any movement your opponent might make, but also be able accurately to reflect the tone of any movement around you. Aikido with mind and body coordinated discipline is designed to train this kind of spiritual state and accurate techniques. It is most difficult to attain such a spiritual condition if all year you keep your spirit in turmoil over matches and contests. This is the third reason why we do not permit them in aikido with mind and body coordinated.

Those who are good at the techniques and strong in the training hall are not always the most useful in genuinely dangerous situations. It is very much like the man who though bright is unable to think of anything at a crucial moment. We know a story of a man, always brave in danger, who, suddenly and unexpectedly coming upon an enemy, was paralyzed with fear at the site of his opponent's sword gleaming before him. Fortunately, the enemy too was startled and unable to move. With some difficulty the first man downed his opponent. Poeple whose spirits in ordinary life are untrained frequently react this way in a crisis. A man is useful when the chips are down only if he studies the principles of the universal in daily life and maintains a firm view of the world and an absolutely immovable spirit.

Chapter *17* | The Unity of Calm and Action

Thinking that calm and action are diametric opposites, many people may consider the very idea of the unity of calm and action strange. Ultimately, however, the two unite. All true aikido with mind and body coordinated techniques demand that the person performing them be in that state of unity between calm and action.

Among the disciplines of calm inactivity we might mention seated Zen meditation, breathing methods, quietly sitting, and praying, among active disciplines, of course, the martial arts and the sports, and physical labor itself. People who engage mainly in the quiet disciplines easily fall into the habit of reverencing calm only and of arriving in a state of the calm that is dead. On the other hand, those who practice only the active disciplines respect only activity and easily become frenzied in their bustling about.

Though in speech we make the distinction between calm and activity, since both are processes born of the *ki* of the universal, fundamentally they are the same. Either state implies the existence of the other. Action within calm, or calm within action, mean that a state of complete calm implies the element of extremely violent activity and that violent activity, by its own nature, implies absolute calm.

As we sit perfectly still we imagine that we are in a state of complete calm, but the fact is, seated on the surface of the revolving earth, we are travelling at great speeds. All of our calm includes this much activity.

Tops that children often play with approach a state of calm stability the faster they spin. We might say that their most perfect state of calm is reached when they move at the greatest speed. The truest calm must contain the nature of the most rapid movement. This is what we mean by action within calm. True calm is not merely sitting still and allowing your consciousness to grow vague. A state of that sort makes wasted time of any attempts to practice seated Zen meditation or breathing methods. If you feel that this is the condition you are about to fall into as you practice some calm discipline, it is much preferable to fall asleep and get a good supply of the *ki* of the universal.

We must be able to instantaneously move with great speed even though, to outward appearances, we remain perfectly calm. We are able to move most rapidly and violently when we are most calm. If even when you confront your opponent's naked sword you remain clear-minded and as calm as the surface of a lake, you can immediately move in accordance with any action your opponent makes. The man who fusses with tricks and frantic devices is not worth mentioning. The man who is so calm that his opponent cannot predict his next move is formidable indeed.

Maintaining a profound calm within even the most violent action is also essential. Like the sea whose lower depths are always peaceful whatever tempest furrows its surface and like the eye of the typhoon around which the violent winds howl, we must always retain our own calm. Strength of action is born from inner calm. For this reason, if we have that calm, regardless of how rapidly we act, we will not upset our breathing. A person who has not mastered this calm will disrupt his breathing, and even a little activity will dull the action of his limbs. Though a man may be ordinarily highly skilled at his techniques, if his breathing is uneven he cannot perform them. If he is facing one man, his opponent will lose control of his breathing too, and everything will be all right. If, however, he is fighting four or five men, if his breathing is rough, he will soon find himself unable to move at all. We must always be conscious of the great importance of preserving our calm in action and of controlling our breathing.

To master action in calm and calm in action you must concentrate all of your spirit in the one point in the lower abdomen. When the one point is infinitely condensed by half, for the first time unity of calm and action is obtained. Whether you are active or still, if you keep your mind and body unified, you will have mastered the secret of unity of calm and action. When you have achieved this state you will be able to handle whatever complexities the world may offer with equanimity and accuracy.

Chapter *18* | Rules for Disciplinants

Training in the Ki Society consists of Ki Class (Shin-Shin-Toitsu-Do, Ki Development) and Aikido with Mind & Body Coordinated Class (Shin-Shin-Toitsu-Aikido).

I. Ki Class

1. Tohei style Ki Unification

It teaches Ki Principles and the Four Basic Principles to Unify Mind & Body.

2. Tohei style Ki Meditations

In order to master the one point in the lower abdomen more fully, the one point is infinitely condensed by half in Tohei style Ki Meditations. Tohei Style Ki Meditations enable us to master the unity of calmness and action and the divine spirit.

3. Tohei sytle Ki Breathing Methods

One is taught to breathe according to the principles of unification of mind and body. One can learn the cardinal principle of living a long and healthy life.

4. Tohei style Ki Exercises

Dead calmness is not the real calmness. Calmness in action is the real clamness. One practises how to maintain coordination of mind and body in his daily activities.

5. Massage with Ki (Kiatsu)

Once you have mastered the true human power, you can also master how to cure diseases. When a pump is not working, priming water must be poured into it before water flows out. In the same way your *ki* flows into the diseased body to prime it to overcome the disease and enable that body to activate its life power.

The above five items are taught in Ki Class. Since we do not practice throwing techniques, even elderly people and sick people can attend it. Such people need the power of mind and body unification.

II. Aikido with Mind and Body Coordinated Class (Shin-Shin-Toitsu-Aikido)

Young people should train the body which contains the mind. Good food must be put into a good vessel. Many people do not know the method of training the body and thus train it without any theory. Such training is harmful to the body.

Aikido with Mind and Body Coordinated training is to train every movement according to the principles of the universal, the Four Basic Principles to Unify Mind and Body, to throw and be thrown. Aikido with Mind and Body Coordinated training is reasonable so that there is no chance to get hurt. Eldery people and children can train themselves without worry.

Before you move or throw others, you are supposed to move the mind. If you can move the mind of others, the body is obliged to follow the mind. Before you lead the mind of others, you must be able to control your own mind and body freely. That is why you have to train yourself with the Four Basic Principles to Unify Mind and Body. Unification of mind and body without movement is rather easy. Unification during motion is difficult. It is more difficult when you are in difficulty or being attacked by others. Aikido with Mind and Body Coordinated trains us to overcome such situations. During the training the principles of the Ki Class are applied and practiced.

I. BE CANDID

Not just in *ki* training, but when you are learning anything, frankness is essential. Some people, ruined by their previous experience or knowledge, are unable to learn things openly. These people have what we call bad habits. They judge things solely on the basis of their own narrow experience and think that what suits them is correct and what does not suit them is wrong. Progress does not lie this way.

Say we have a glass full of water. If we try to pour more water into it, the water will flow out, and only a little will remain in the glass. Once empty the glass, and it will hold plenty of new water. If your head is crammed with this and that, whatever new things you try to learn, they will not go in. Being frank and candid is a good way to empty your head of the useless stuff in it. *Ki* training is the discipline that lets you make great progress in moving from a world that emphasizes the body to one that centers on the spirit, from one that thinks in dualities, to one that thinks in absolutes, and from a world of fighting to a world of peace. It is as if you were passing from the world of sound waves into a world of supersonics.

If you do not use all humility in studying *ki* it will not stay with you.

Some people decide once and for all in their heart that they are not going to believe what anyone says. Perhaps they feel that, if they are not suspicious of everything, someone will dupe them. Everything has both a positive and a negative interpretation. Constant suspicion encourages only negative interpretations and the inability to think well even of good things.

It is also dangerous, however, to believe everything you hear because you cannot know where such credulity will lead you. Still the man who is convinced that he can doubt everything in the world must lead a life of doubting himself as well.

A young woman teacher whom I met in America asked me to tell her about *ki*. I explained the idea that the mind controls the body and the principle of the unbendable arm. I then had her tense her arm as much as possible, and I bent it. She said, "You can bend my arm because you are strong and I am weak." "Very well," I said, "This time do not tense your arm, but think with all your being that your own spirit's strength is flowing out a thousand miles ahead." She seemed to be doing as I asked, but I could still bend her arm. I was attempting to convey a fact. I was able to bend her arm because she would not think as I asked her. When I asked her to think sincerely of what she was doing she said that she had been sincere, but in repeated trials I always was able to bend her arm. Since further explanation would have been useless, I asked another woman standing by to help us. I asked her first to tense her arm. She did, and the woman teacher was able to bend it. Next I asked our new assistant to relax her arm and to concentrate on her spiritual strength's flying forward a thousand miles. I then had the teacher try to bend her arm, but she could not. The second woman said, "This is wonderful, I understand exactly." The teacher insisted that she could not bend the other woman's arm because the other woman was stronger, though in fact the teacher was the larger of the two. I said that the teacher had been able to bend her arm when she had tensed it, and the teacher replied, "She let me bend it on purpose." Though the second woman denied that this was true, the teacher stubbornly refused to believe her. I saw no sense in explaining further. If the conversation had been in Japanese I might have gone on, but my poor English was not up to the task.

The Bible teaches that those who believe are blessed. People of this teacher's sort are themselves inviting unhappiness. I can only wonder what sort of psychology she teaches in the classroom. Her own cup is full of old water, and no new water can get in.

Though this teacher was an extreme case, to a greater or lesser extent her type is common. People of this kind are delaying their own progress. Positive thinking and negative thinking are different, but many people confuse the two. If we take off our colored glasses and think straight, we can tell for ourselves what is correct and what is mistaken. It is fine to study and learn a great deal, but it is foolish to delay one's own progress by wandering off on the side paths of suspicion. In *ki* training a frank candid person makes progress all the faster for that reason.

2.   PERSEVERE

If you begin something you must see it through. If you are doing something just for fun it is all right to try a little here and a little there, but once you decide that this is the path you are going to follow, it is wrong to break off midway. To do so only proves the weakness of your will power.

Although in some cases working conditions or other limitations make it impossible to continue something you have begun, since *ki* training carries over into daily life, and since you always have your own mind and body with you, you have no excuse for quitting it.

Whatever you decide to study, you are going to run into some stone walls along the way. Simply starting something and leaving off right away is a separate issue because in cases like that the person never really intends to go very far anyway, but sometimes people, really wanting to continue, give up when they encounter some difficulty. Depending on the person involved, some give up *ki* training after a month or two, and some last as long as six months. Usually a person who lasts a year will do it for a long time. In other words, it takes about a year to get a good taste of what *ki* training is really like. People who quit after about a month, and complain and criticize it, do so because they themselves do not understand it well.

No matter how big the bell, if you only tap it, it can give out only a faint sound. We must understand thoroughly that the weakness of the blow, not a fault of the bell, makes the sound poor. It is much the same way in the old story of the blind men and the elephant. Each, unable to feel all of the beast, judged an elephant to be only the part he examined. The man who touched the leg said an elephant was a tall column, and the man who felt the trunk said an elephant was like a long pole. Individually none of the blind men was wrong, but what each described as an elephant was nowhere near the real thing. Unless we can see the entire thing, we cannot understand what we are dealing with.

Lately some people have been purporting to teach a collection of all the good points from judo, karate, and kenpo. All is well and good if they are really teaching all the good points, but we must bear in mind that what they present is much like the elephant according to the blind men. It is nothing like the real thing. It is not easy to investigate any one thing thoroughly, particularly in the case of *ki* training, which involves studying the laws of the universal and actually putting them to practice. We must be fully aware of the fact that *ki* training is something we continue throughout life. Maintaining the one point in the lower abdomen, relaxing, and preserving positive *ki* are parts of the comfortable and pleasant life attitude that most suits nature. It is an indispensable factor in developing your personality, in making of yourself a splendid member of society. To continue it all your life is the correct path to follow.

We encounter troubles in our discipline too. We feel somehow stiffled, or we get fed up. Sometimes a weak-willed self-satisfied person will give up. Actually, if we do not complain or attempt to jusify ourselves but continue to practice patiently we can surmount any difficulties. Once we have knocked down the wall in our path our vision expands, things become more interesting, and we make steady progress. When we come to the next obstacle, we will be ready to knock that down, and continue forward. Optimistically consider each new obstacle as proof that you have progressed that far along the way. As an old saying has it, we only approach real faith as faith repeatedly overcomes doubt.

3. DIFFERENCES IN TECHNIQUES AND TEACHING METHODS

I want to take this chance to set at rest beginners who often ask, "Just whom shall I listen to? Techniques and teaching methods vary with the instructor and lead astray those of us who are new."

Bathed in the same sun and blessed with the same rains, trees grow and flourish differently according to their own characteristics. Though we all follow the same basic *ki* principles, depending on the personality involved, the teaching methods differ and the techniques themselves assume a slightly different cast. Of course, we are not discussing techniques that clearly depart from the basic principles of *ki*, but if the techniques do conform to these principles we need not consider differences among them strange.

Aikido with mind and body coordinated is made up of techniques that express the nature of the universe through the whole human body. Just as the universal itself varies into spring, summer, autumn, and winter, so some techniques are gentle like spring breezes, and some are severe like the frosts of autumn. They can alter freely with the time and the place. Generally, the beginner practices the gentle techniques, but as he grows and his body develops he comes to the point where he can carry out the more severe ones. Consequently, A can teach the spring-like techniques and B the autumn ones, and if they both follow the principles of *ki*, both are correct.

We sometimes say, "See the person, then explain the rule." That is, teaching methods vary according to the student's experience of discipline, his age, and his personality. Often in aikido with mind and body coordinated training we have a wide mixture of the young, the old, men, women, the experienced and the inexperienced. In cases of this sort the teaching methods will depend on which level the instructor decides to emphasize. Just as many paths can lead to the top of a mountain, so many methods of explaining can lead to an understanding of a single technique.

For example , A might say in explaining the unbendable arm, "Concentrate on your *ki*'s passing through your arm and extending to the end of the universal," whereas B, after explaining the one point in the lower abdomen and having him raise his arm might say, "Think of nothing at all." One man says think and the other says think of nothing. Common sense tells us that these two are direct opposites, and that both A and B are deceiving the beginner. The fact is, however, that no contradiction exists. Both A and B are correct because sending forth *ki* and maintaining the one point in the lower abdomen are the same thing.

For these reasons techniques and teaching methods vary, but the beginner should listen to what his instructor frankly tells him as he practices. If the student listens with a cool head, he will know if a technique does not agree with the principles of *ki*. If it does not, he should not learn it. Instructors vary in experience and sometimes misunderstand things. More rarely we find instructors who are conceited or who attempt to teach their own brand of techniques, but as the beginner practices he will become aware of what conforms to the principles and what does not.

Just learning the theory of *ki* is not enough. Because you must repeatedly train until you have refined both your mind and your body regardless of who your instructor is, it is important to practice as devotedly as you can. Remember, people who do nothing but criticize are generally the slowest to make progress.

4. BE BOTH PUPIL AND INSTRUCTOR

Finally I want you to understand that as you are still learning you are also teaching it.

Though if you only halfway learn something, the fine points go in one ear and out the other, in the case of the *ki* principle of mind and body unification, a turn of the neck or of the finger can have great meaning and make a great difference in the effect of a technique. Sometimes,though try as you may you cannot down your opponent, a change in the way you bend your finger will make downing him quite easy. Though a turn in the neck or finger is so easy that we take no notice of it, since these turns involve directional shifts in the flow of *ki* they are very important.

If you learn something with the idea of rushing home and teaching it to your brother or someone else you will pay particular attention, listen carefully and make sure you master it well. If you always practice with the idea in mind that someday you might have to teach what you are learning your progress will be even faster.

Though *ki* training is learning the rules of the universal and putting them into practice, the majority of the people of this world do not know these rules. If today you learn one of them, at least one more human knows that one rule. In addition to that you have become a teacher with a qualification to teach others. If you learn the unbendable arm today you are in a position to explain and teach it to anyone tomorrow.

How much finer qualifications to teach in this world will you have once you have disciplined yourself to the point where you can actually apply the laws of the universal!

If each man would study with the knowledge that he will become a leader of scoiety and will be able to make his contribution, the world would become that much brighter.

Chapter *19* | Rules for Instructors

It is easier to learn than to teach. It is easy enough just to explain something without caring whether the person learning understands or not, but if you really lead correctly and teach impartially with a desire to make your students master the material, taking into consideration all the while each person's individual characteristics and learning habits, it is no easy matter. Teaching *ki* is particularly difficult because in doing so we must raise a person from the world of the body to the world of the spirit, we must teach mind and body unification and lead our students to the point where they can put what we teach into actual practice.

Of course it stands to reason that the teacher must have mastered, put into practice, and believe what he teaches. If we teach the rules of the universal incorrectly, just as when the blind lead the blind, there is no telling what mistaken path we may follow. To teach we must keep our own eyes wide open and accept full responsibility for what we are doing.

I. GROWING TOGETHER

Sometimes in *ki* training we encounter people who practice diligently but who are interested only in their own progress and look displeased when they are asked to lead their juniors. Enthusiastic discipline is fine, of course, but if only the techniques progress, people with a self-centered attitude can reach a certain point, the point at which the body can progress, but they will be unable to enter the realm of spiritual progress. The basic principle of *ki* is love and protection of all things. Our spirits are one with the spirit of the universal. For this reason our *ki* is in a state of perfect conflux with the universal's *ki*. The attitude that, "I'm perfectly all right," selfishness, in other words, is an obstruction to the flow of *ki* , and prevents our being able to really receive into ourselves the true principles of the universal. In addition, selfishness leads directly to conceit, which in turn retards progress.

In general, in this world there is no such thing as "for the sake of other people." We often decide to do something to the best of our ability for others so as to gain their gratitude and then get angry when things do not work out exactly as we planned. All things done for the sake of others are actually for our own sakes. We do them largely to increase our own virtue. After all, are we ourselves not the ones who profit most by becoming better when we exert our best efforts for others? The man in *ki* training who studies this principle most diligently and who does most to lead his juniors along the road of technical and spiritual progress is the man who advances the farthest.

The other material arts teach that we will not gain strength unless we always train against people that are stronger than us. Although aikido with mind and body coordinated also teaches that it is very important to encounter people stronger and more outstanding than ourselves and to learn from them all that we can, it also maintains that practice of this kind alone is insufficient. Aikido with mind and body coordinated holds that we should first master something by ourselves and then, to the limits of our knowledge, attempt to kindly lead our juniors along the same path. We progress by teaching others because teaching is a form of learning. A person teaching correct principles should not himself make errors. If he tells others not to be angry, he should not lose his own temper. We must do as we instruct others and in correcting the bad habits of other people correct our own as well.

Though it is very difficult to train a person who is slow to learn and who has many bad habits to the point where he can perform techniques correctly, if we kept him always in sight and try, basing our work on correct principles, to teach him at least something, he will develop. Simultaneously, the man who instructs will always make great progress himself in the techniques he teaches and in the finer points of the *ki* principles.

The pupil will, of course, be very grateful, but the instructor must also be thankful for the chance to gain more good discipline. By earnestly and kindly attempting to lead others we make great strides in our own techniques and in our own personality.

It is wrong to believe that we ourselves cannot achieve a position higher than other people if we do not suppress others. It is a fine thing to progress oneself by causing another to make progress. The way of *ki* is to learn with your companion, progress with him, and help him. This is certainly a good path to follow in the world as well.

Do not be stingy with a technique you have learned. Locking up the principles you learn from the universal in your own private heart is no way to receive further blessings. We must love without stinting. If we give of what we have learned as much as we can we can learn still more. Do not worry that the supply will be exhausted, the universal is infinite.

2. AN INSTRUCTOR MUST BE MODEST

Sometimes people in the instructor's seat want to swagger a bit. The truth is that just because someone is teaching he has not necessarily mastered all of the principles the universal has to teach. He may be a step further advanced but he is still a fellow traveller with his students on the universal road. After all, the person who has stepped out ahead must lead those who are behind.

For an instructor to consider himself a perfected being is a ridiculous illusion. Conceit closes the eyes of the spirit and leads to regression rather than to progress. Be negligent, and more and more the younger group will push you to the background. Though a great teacher propounds it, a mistake is still a mistake; and though a beginner performs it, a correct act is still correct. It is not for the instructor to be satisfied with the reputation of sitting in the leader's chair, he must be constantly in search of correct progress. A man becomes a splendid teacher only when he is the possessor of a humble heart.

3. PUPILS ARE THE TEACHER'S MIRROR

While the pupil and the teacher are fellow travellers on the universal road they are also a double mirror in that each reflects the other. The virtues and faults of the teacher are visible in the pupil and vice versa. If the pupil sincerely studies, the teacher will teach with sincerity, and the two can mature and progress together. If a student is disrespectful to the teacher or shows interest in learning the techniques only, the teacher will know it, and the student will be unable to learn the best the teacher has to offer. Even when the teacher is completely sincere in his instruction, a student with this kind of attitude is unlikely to take it in effectively.

Once you make up your mind to study under a certain instructor, do not use your immature spirit to criticize him. Study so enthusiastically that it will seem as if you have even assumed his habits.

Naturally, the teacher's spirit reflects in his students. If a teacher is conceited, his students will be, too. If he swaggers, so will they. If he regards them lightly, they will return the feeling. A teacher who explains correct *ki* principles, however, and puts them into practice, will develop good pupils. If the teacher is the pupils' mirror, so are they his. A teacher who finds bad habit among his students, should regard them as reflections of his own. The image a teacher sees in his pupils in an admonition to him to continue his efforts even more strenuously.

An instructor who teaches the principles of the universal must not forget that the students are observing him. His own words and actions must conform to the principle of unified words and action that he expounds. It is vital to preserve the attitude that he can learn from his students.

4. RIGHT NOT MIGHT

Though it is good that an instructor teaches his students to become strong, strength should not be his sole aim. The attitude that might is right is certainly unpraiseworthy. As the number of people professing the rule of might increases in the world, so does disorder and the danger of war. In *ki* training, where the goal is unification of mind and body and the perfection of the human personality, even a little of the desire for power or complacency that one knows all of the techniques is disgraceful and demands correction. Aikido with mind and body coordinated contains thousands of techniques and tens of thousands of variations on them. Once you have learned a certain amount and are enlightened as to the principles of *ki* you yourself can devise new techniques and uncover new movements, but this is possible only if the principles you follow are the correct ones.

Some people think that if they devise some different technique, try it on someone, and find that it works, they have actually created a new technique. Just as when an adult tries a technique on a child, whether the adult does it properly or not he is likely to win, so if a man with four or five years' experience tries a technique on a beginner, the more experienced man is sure to win. The problem is not whether the technique works but whether it is correct. An incorrect technique will not work even on a beginner who has made only a little progress.

A few instructors like to have their students try a technique on them so that they can put them down and show how strong they are. A teacher should correct his student's bad points, but he should not halt their technical development midway. If he tries to show off his own strength he will certainly arouse resistance among his students. He will not be teaching the principle of non-dissension but the theory of battle. The students will lose the heart to seek the correct way and will desire strength alone. Always humbly attempt to conform what you are teaching to the correct principles, and avoid anything that does not. Your teaching attitude must always be a quest for what conforms to the principles and a desire to teach those things to others.

It is not the mighty man who is right, but the man in the right who is mighty. Though we hear that among the men in the right there are weak men, those who are weak are actually not completely in the right. The path that conforms to the law of the universal is the way to the greatest strength. We must exert all of our efforts proving this and to showing to the world that right is might.

5.   ATTITUDE NOT SENIORITY MAKES AN INSTRUCTOR

The notion exists that one cannot teach until he himself has become strong. Some people with more experience refuse to instruct their juniors because they feel that they themselves are immature and weak. Strength and technical skill and being a good instructor are different questions. The strong person is not always a good instructor. Of course, all is well if a man is both strong and a good instructor, but he can be weaker and not terribly skilful at the techniques himself and still successfully teach others. A man does not have to be a wonderful swimmer to be a good swimming coach.

To become a good instructor one must kindly and enthusiastically teach others the basic principles to the limits of his mastery. Learn for one day or one year, and you will be able to be a splendid teacher of what you learned in that day or year.

Let us say that A asks B how to get to town C. B himself has never been there, but he has heard that one should go straight ahead. If he says, "I've never been to C, and I have no right to tell you how to get there," it is the same as the man who declines to instruct another in some *ki* point because he feels he is immature. Such an answer is straightforward and modest, but scarcely kind. B might better have said, "I've never been, but I hear that you can get there by going straight ahead." If you have studied and believe the laws of the universal you need have no hesitations about saying, "I myself am immature, but this is what I have learned. Let's train together." Since the universal is infinite if you wait until you have mastered it all to teach others, you will never do any teaching. When it comes right down to it, we are all immature. The fine instructors are those who, with a true faith, attempt to walk the path of progress together with others.

A man, about 50 years old, who had just made the first *dan* in aikido with mind and body coordinated moved from Hawaii to Guam and asked me how he could continue his training. There was no training hall on Guam. I told him that he would make great progress himself if he gathered a group of his friends together and taught them what he knew. He objected that he was too immature and lacked sufficient confidence to teach others. I explained to him that I, though immature, teach others because the path I have followed is a universal and correct one. If he believed that what he had learned was true he should be able to teach others also.

I explained that the people he would teach would not know so much as the unbendable arm and that if he taught it to them, he could not tell how much it might help each in his own way. If he learned one day, he could teach what he learned that one day, and since he had learned all the time leading up to his reaching the first *dan*, there was no reason why he could not instruct. Though I pursuaded him that no one need hesitate to teach the way of the universal, he came straight out with this question: "What will I say if someone larger and stronger than I comes along?" I said that he should praise the person for being so strong and tell him that as he grew older his strength would fail. Teach the strong man that he needs to train his mind because it is the mind that controls the body. I told him to say, "Bodily strength is limited. I am immature yet and at over fifty years of age not very strong, but I am studying ways to train my mind and I intend to make plenty of progress from now on. The aikido with mind and body coordinated I am learning is the true path of the universal. If you will follow me and learn too you will become even stronger. As you grow older you will progress. You will correct your bad habits and improve your personality. I am in the midst of learning now; why don't we train together?" I told the man that if he were to talk this way, the strong man would probably happily join in with him.

Several years later, I received a photograph of him, small and seated in a chair, with a large group of his students, some of them twice his size, all around him. They are all deeply fond of him as their respected teacher.

Aikido with mind and body coordinated can come to nothing if a person foolishly imitates the techniques alone. Only when each technique, each bodily movement, conforms with the principles will we find true aikido with mind and body coordinated in which the mind and body are one. For this reason, to spread it we must collect together really fine teachers and send them to every land, but we need men with true understanding of the basic *ki* principles and men with a true spirit more than we need powerful experts in the techniques.

6.   BE FAIR AND IMPARTIAL

A teacher must be completely disinterested, kind, fair, and impartial to all students. Since teaching is learning, if you have selfishness in your heart, your teaching will not be good self-training. On the contrary, I must warn you that it will only breed further selfishness and bad habits.

Of course, it is easy to teach people who learn fast, but we must not overlook those that no other martial art would accept, the people who are earnest but who have bad habits and who are slow to learn. The aikido with mind and body coordinated instructor must be impartial to all. A person whose body is inflexible and clumsy or who does not learn fast is doubtless using his mind and his body incorrectly. For instance, a man whose body does not move as lithely as it should is doubtless either stopping his flow of *ki* or pulling his *ki* inward. Teach him to send his *ki* forth and his body will become more flexible. A man who is slow to pick things up probably is neglecting to concentrate his mind. He lives with the idea that his mind and his body are separate entities and thus cannot make his body do what his mind wants it to do.

Though there may be other basic factors involved in these cases, if we correct these points. and set the person on the right path, he can develop into a fine man. Anyone can teach a man who is good at anything he tries A man who can teach those who really need teaching is truly an ehthusiastic instructor. Moreover, by striving and devising ways to teach others, the instructor himself gets fine discipline in the basic principles of leadership and in the finer points of *ki* principles.

Impartiality does not mean that you have to teach everyone the same way. Some people learn something the first time they hear it, others do not get it down after ten repetitions. Because older people, women, and girls do not usually get much exercise they may be slower to learn, and the instructor must be particularly careful of them and see that more experienced students help them during practice.

It is important for experienced students to practice among themselves, but they must realize that leading their juniors is equally important to their own training and discipline.

This is the way to become a truly impartial instructor, a man illuminated by the spirit of love and affection for all, a man with compassion for everyone.

7.   INSTRUCTORS MUST WORK TOGETHER

Instructors must not squabble among themselves over techniques and teaching methods. In the same technique many methods exist, and the technique varies in accordance with the way an opponent applies force. All of them are correct if they adhere to the basic principles of *ki*. I myself have taught a technique one way in one country and another in another. At times, my movements alter in accordance with the way an opponent applies force. Explaining all of this in detail is the most correct way, but since there are so many aikido techniques, if we delved into the complete details of one of them we would have no time to teach the others.

Regardless of how many ways I teach a technique, invaribaly one person will remember only way *a* and another only way *b*. The two will then fight accusing each other of doing the technique wrong. Aikido with mind and body coordinated techniques have a slightly different cast depending on the individual involved. In some cases we use the milder techniques, in other the more severe ones, and in many cases the way of teaching alters in accordance with the pupil's degree of advancement. All of this is confusing enough to the beginner, but if the instructors argue and accuse each other of mistaken practices, the beginner will be in a quandary over what to do and with whom to study.

Once, after a lapse of about a year, I returned to visit a training hall where I had formerly taught. I found there A and B arguing over who was performing a certain technique correctly.Each said that the way he learned the technique was correct and that the other's way was wrong. I had them perform the technique for me and said that both were correct. They were troubled over this decision, though to tell the truth neither of them performed the technique very well. I told them that though both were right, both were also wrong. Since they looked as if they did not believe me, I explained: "Both of you perform the technique correctly. I am sure that I taught A to do it his way and B to do it his way. I say you are both right because each of you remembered one of the two correct ways. Both are mistaken because your poor postures cause the technique to go badly." After I had actually shown them what they were doing wrong, both of them could do the technique perfectly well.

I then explained that if instructors quarrel among themselves, they will mislead the students. No one who learns ten things will remember all ten of them. Instructors must study together selflessly and listen to what their companions have to say so that they can all understand the correct way. I also pointed out that if they had spent the same amount of time in mutual cooperation on the disputed point that they had wasted on arguing, they would have discovered their mistake before I ever arrived at the hall.

From time to time, instructors should get together for a modest and open study period. They should discuss not only whether a technique works, but also whether it agrees with *ki* principles. Just as moving water follows certain laws, so does the flow of *ki*. Any attempt to force it to alter its course is unnatural. If the technique under discussion actually conforms to the principles, whether you throw your opponent or are thrown by him, the technique should feel right. If it does not, something in it is out of harmony with the principles, and you should reexamine all of its points.

Never stick to your opinion only because you have always done so. Always correct immediately what is found wrong. When sometimes the elders are mistaken and the younger men right, the elders may not want to give in and follow their juniors. In fact, by correcting their mistake they will not be so much following their juniors as simply doing the right thing. The younger people will invariably trust an elder who frankly admits, "I have made a mistake." Failure to admit a mistake will make the younger men suspicious of everything one does and earn their distrust.

The universal is broad, and its rules are deep. Always be modest, always strive to learn all the universal can teach, and always lend an ear to what people have to say. Teacher or student, elder, or junior, right is right, and a mistake is a mistake. Engrave this thought on your hearts.

These rules for instructors apply to all phases of society. We are followers and instructors. A good follower will always be a good instructor and vice versa. A man who is sincere in life will always be a good leader in life. My wish is that all would give vital application to the basic principles of *ki*, train and make actual proof of your training at the training halls, and go into the world to become active and influential leaders.

Conclusion

CONCLUSION

In the first part of this book I explained the basic principle of *ki* and in the second gave some examples of how we can apply these principles to our training and to our daily lives. This book, however, is too small and its author not far enough advanced to explain all of the universal in its immensity. All that we can say is that the man who studies aikido with mind and body coordinated bases his thinking on these principles and, silently facing the enormous universal, disciplines himself in this way.

To speak of the great road of the universal is in no way strange or peculiar, for a road is actually there under the feet of anyone who wishes to use it. A person who first sees a small man trained in aikido with mind and body coordinated throwing someone twice his size, or comfortably dealing with four or five other men, probably considers it is all very strange because he is thinking only in terms of the laws of the body and seeing it only with the body's eyes. Were he to realize that the mind controls the body and view the case from the standpoint of the laws of the spirit, he would see that it is in no way marvelous. Of course, it requires training, but since there is a principle for throwing people, to be able to throw people is only natural. Those who study *ki* can do these things because they are following the great road of the universal. Anyone who wants to can do likewise.

Just training at the training hall and being able to apply techniques to your opponents is not the entire great road of the universal. The road is the only one that humans must follows, and it extends to everything we do.

Of course, training hall practice is important, but it is not the only method. One only knows true *ki* principles if he maintains the one point in the lower abdomen, makes the conflux of *ki* with that of the universal part and parcel of his daily life, is able to make free use of *ki*, and applies the principles of *ki* to everything he does.

If a person refuses to recognize a hardship no hardship exists. Confirm yourself and your relation with the universal, and the rough waves of this world will loose their fearsomeness. My wish is to make of this priceless gift of life something truer, stronger, and happier so that we can walk boldly through the world and make our own contribution to its betterment. I have written this book in the hope that it will help spread *ki* to all the corners of the world and increase, even if only one more person, the number of *ki* followers.

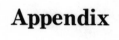

Appendix

THIRTEEN RULES
FOR DISCIPLINANTS

1. *Ki* training reveals to us the path to oneness with the universal. To co-ordinate mind and body and become one with nature itself is the chief purpose of *ki* training.

2. As nature loves and protects all creation and help all things grow and develop, so we must teach every student with sincerity and without discrimination or partiality.

3. There is no discord in the absolute truth of the universal, but there is discord in the realm of relative truth. To contend with others and win brings only a relative victory. Not to contend and yet win brings absolute victory. To gain only a relative victory sooner or later leads to inevitable defeat. While you are practicing to become strong, learn how you can avoid fighting. By learning to throw your opponent and enjoy it and to be thrown and enjoy that too and by helping one another in learning the correct techniques you will progress very rapidly.

4. Do not criticize any of the other matrial arts. The mountain does not laugh at the river because it is lowly, nor does the river speak ill of the mountain because it cannot move about. Everyone has his own characteristics and gains his own position in life. Speak ill of others, and it will surely come back to you.

5. The martial arts begin and end with courtesy, not in form alone, but in heart and mind as well. Respect the teacher who teaches you and do not cease to be grateful especially to the founder who shows the way. He who neglects this should not be surprised if his students make light of him.

6. Be warned against conceit. Conceit not only halts your progress, it causes you to regress. Nature is boundless, its principles are profound. What brings conceit? It is brought on by shallow thinking and a cheaply-bought compromise with your ideals.

7. Cultivate the calm mind that comes from making the universal a part of the body by concentrating your thoughts on the one point in the lower abdomen. You must know that it is a shame to be narrow-minded. Do not dispute with others merely to defend your own views. Right is right, wrong is wrong. Judge calmly what is right and what is wrong. If you are convinced that you are wrong, manfully make amends. If you meet one who is your superior, joyfully accept his teaching. If any man is in error, quietly explain to him the truth, and strive to make him

understand.

8. Even a one-inch worm has a half-inch of spirit. Every man respects his own ego. Do not, therefore, slight anyone, nor hurt his self-respect. Treat a man with respect, and he will respect you. Make light of him, and he will make light of you. Respect his personality and listen to his views, and he will gladly follow you.

9. Do not become angry. If you become angry it shows that your mind has wandered from the one point in the lower abdomen. Anger is something to be ashamed of in *ki* training. Do not become angry on your own account. Be angry only when the rights of nature or of your country are endangered. Concentrate on the one point, and become angry all over. Know that he who is easily angered loses courage at important moments.

10. Spare no effort when you teach. You advance as your students advance. Do not be impatient when you teach. No one can learn everything well at one time. Perseverance is important in teaching, as are patience, kindness, and the ability to put yourself in your students' place.

11. Do not be a haughty instructor. The students grow in knowledge as they obey their teacher. It is the special characteristic of training in *ki* that the teacher also advances by teaching his students. Training requires an atmosphere of mutual respect between teacher and students. If you see a haughty man, you see a shallow thinker.

12. In practicing do not show your strength without some good purpose lest you awaken resistance in the minds of those who are watching you. Do not argue about strength, but teach the right way. Words alone cannot explain. Sometimes by being the one to be thrown, you can teach more effectively. Do not halt your student's throw at midpoint or stop his *ki* before he can complete a movement, or you will give him bad habits.

13. Do whatever you do with conviction. We study thoroughly the principle of the universal and practice it, and the universal protects us. We have nothing to be doubtful or to fear. Real conviction comes from the belief that we are one with the universal. We must have the courage to say with Confucius: If I have an easy conscience, I dare to face an enemy of ten thousand men.

KI NO KENKYUKAI H. Q.
Ushigome Heim 101, 2-30 Hara-machi, Shinjuku-ku, Tokyo

Tel: 03-353-3461

Branches of KI NO KENKYUKAI

Honolulu Ki Society, Mr. Seiichi Tabata
2003 Nuuanu Ave. Honolulu, HI 96817 U.S.A.

Tel: 808-521-3513

Big Island Ki Society, Mr. Takashi Nonaka
P O.Box 438, Papaikou, HI 96781, U.S.A.

Tel: 808-964-1480

Maui Aikido Ki Society, Mr. Shinichi Suzuki
P.O.Box 724 Wailuku, Maui, HI 96793 U.S.A.

Kauai Ki Society, Mr. Tetsuji Masumura
2901 Pua Loke St. Lihue, Kauai, HI 96766 U.S. A.

New Jersey Ki Society, Mr. Terrence Pierce
529 Howard Street, Riverton, N.J. 08077, U.S.A.

Virginia Ki Society, Mr. George Simcox
5631 Cornish Way, Alexandria, VA. 22310, U.S.A.

Montgomery County Ki Society, Mr. Daniel Frank
19004 Rolling Acres Way, Olney, MD 20832 U.S.A.

Chicago Ki. Society, Mr. Jonathan Ely
7721, S. Luella,Chicago, IL 60649, U.S.A.

Tel: 312-478-4464

Arizona Ki Society, Mr. Kirk Fowler
8306 East Welsh Trail Scottsdale, AZ 85258 U.S.A.

Tel: 602-991-3117

Midland Ki Society Federation, Mr. Koichi Kashiwaya
P.O.Box 818, Boulder, CO 80306, U.S.A.

Tel: 303-442-0505

Northwest Ki Society Federation, Mr. Calvin Yutaka Tabata
P.O.Box 02025, Portland, OR 97202 U.S.A.

Tel: 503-223-9124

Seattle Ki. Society, Mr. Dick Hansau
6106 Roosevelt Way NE. Seattle, WA. 98115, U.S.A.

Tel: 206-747-0581

Northern California Ki Society Federation, Mr. Hideki Shiohira
130 Willits St. Daly City CA 94014 U.S.A..

Tel: 415-756-8913

Southern California Ki Society, Mr. Masao Shoji
1150 W. 148th St. Gardena CA 90247 U.S.A.

Tel: 213-532-1365

South Carolina Ki Society, Mr. David Eo Shaner
Dept. of Philosophy/Furrman University, Greenville, S.C. 29613
U.S.A.

Ki No Kenkyukai Bruxelles
70 Rue Lieutenant Liedel Bruxelles 1070 Belgium

Tel: 02-5230621

Ki No Kenkyukai ITALIA
Casella P. le 3003, Firenze 26, ITALIA   Tel. 055-362090

Ki-Aikido Dojo Berlin, Mrs. Marion Kranz
Hedemanstr. 11. D-1000 Berlin 61, West Germany   Tel: 030-611 69 39

St. Aikido Sanju ryu, Mr. Eugene Du Long
Lorentzstr. 37, 5223 EW s'Hertogenbosch, Netherlands   Tel: 073-210190

Ki No Kenkyukai Fulham London, Mr. Brian Reeve
70 Waldemar Avenue London SW6 England U.K.   Tel: 736-0800

Ki Society of West Bromwich, Mr. Philip Michael Jones
25 Lyndhurst. Road, West Bromwich, West Midlands, B71 3 JE, England U.K
                                                       Tel: 021-552-6405

Ki Society Coventry, Mr. Philip George Burgess
5 Hopkins Road, Coundon, Coventry England U.K.   Tel: 0203-598147

Stoubridge Ki Society, Mr. Glyn Simcox
11, Tyrol Close, Wollaston, Stoubridge, West Midlands England U.K.
                                                       Tel: 0384-372961

Ki No Kenkyukai Manchester, Dr. K.D. Jones
15 Withington St. Hopwood, Heywood, Lancs U.K. OL10, 2HQ
                                                       Tel: 44-706-68576

Burton Ki Society, Mr. Roy John Cliff
12 Kensington Rd. Winshill, Burton-on-Trent Staffs England U.K.
                                                       Tel: 0283-38138

Leasowes Ki Club, Mr. M. Dipple
74 Bisell Way, Brierley Hill, West Midlands DY5, 2RZ England U.K.
                                                       Tel: 0384-892288

Rhondda Ki Society, Mr. Richard Gardiner
Trederwen Gwaun Bedw, Cymmer, Porth, Rhondda Mid-Glan S. Wales U.K.
                                                       Tel: 0443-683846

Australian Ki Society, Mr. Michael Williams
P.O Box 570, Bryon Bay, New South Wales 2481, Australia   Tel: 07-349-4144

New Zealand Ki Society, Mr. Roger Cruickshank
P.O.Box 1140, Auckland, New Zealand

Ki. Society of the Philippines, Mr. Nestor Perrin
90 Women's Club Street Santol, Quezon City 1113
Philippines   Tel: 61-69-97

Aikido Ki No Kenkyukai Singapore Branch, Mr. Francis H. S. Chong
53 Paterson Road, Singapore 0923 Singapore   Tel: 737-4839

Ki No Kenkyukai Sao Paulo DOJO
Rua Sebastian Carneiro, 501-AP 71 Aclimacao 01543 Sao Paulo-SP Brazil

Ki No Kenkyukai Indonesia, Mr. Takehisa Kinoshita
JL Bendungan Hilir Raya 31, Jakarta 10210 Indonesia   Tel. 5703071